Escaping the Russian Bear

An Estonian Girl's Memoir of Loss and Survival During World War II

by

Kristina von Rosenvinge

LAKESHORE PRESS

Printed in the United States of America

To My Parents

Gunvor Maria and Hans Luts
*Who lost their lives,
casualties of the Russian Bear*

Helga and Werner Toffer
*Whose love for life and freedom
fueled our escapes*

CONTENTS

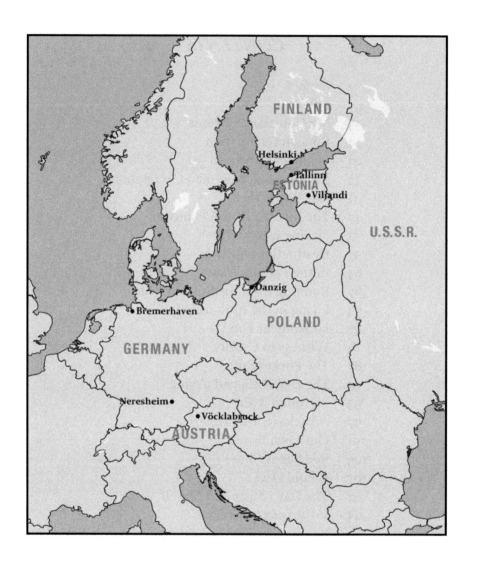

Escaping the Russian Bear

An Estonian Girl's Memoir of Loss and Survival During World War II

PREFACE

The rays of the afternoon sun turn the surface of the water before me into a shimmering dance. I am on a 30-foot inflatable rubber boat perched on a seat as if riding a horse, fiercely gripping the handlebars, for the 14-mile ride from Tallinn, Estonia, out into the Gulf of Finland. We skim across the water at a fast clip. For miles all I can see is water and then, at last, a glimpse of land. As we get closer, I make out a lighthouse and know that this is Keri Island, a place I have longed to go to ever since 1993, when I heard that a memorial had been erected there for the passengers and crew of the Kaleva airplane. It is the closest piece of land to where the plane is believed to have gone down.

The Kaleva was on a routine flight from Estonia to Finland on June 14, 1940, when two Russian airplanes viciously attacked it during what was still peacetime. Having no way to defend itself, the passenger plane burst into flames and plunged into the sea. This attack was the precursor of the invasion that pulled Estonia into World War II and dramatically altered the country's fate. For me this boat ride to Keri Island was a journey of remembrance of my personal loss 73 years ago.

The world I entered in 1938 was comfortable and predictable, much like what my grandchildren have experienced in their own lives. Soon all of that changed as war erupted around us. Of course I was too young to understand the political context of the war and the horror that war creates for the people innocently caught up in it. The war raged in Europe for more than five years—until May 1945—and greatly transformed my life and my homeland, Estonia.

My family came to the United States in 1952 as displaced persons. When I have shared that we fled during the war from Estonia to Germany, astonished reactions greet me:

"How could you go to Hitler's Reich?"
"Didn't you all know what he was doing?"
"Had you not heard about the evils the Nazis were committing?"

These are valid questions, and of course, as an adult living in the United States, I now understand why people believed that the first objective was to defeat Germany. My family during the war, however, was forced to choose between finding a way out of Estonia and facing the horrors of Russian occupation. Germany was the one country that allowed us to enter as war refugees: the doors of all other countries remained closed to us. We yearned for the end of the war so that we could return to Estonia. That was not to be. Estonia did not regain independence after the war, and until 1991 it was a Soviet Socialist Republic of the Union of Soviet Socialist Republics.

I have limited this memoir to the years including and right after World War II, stopping after we crossed the Atlantic Ocean on our journey to America, since that is the beginning of a new chapter in my life. I want my grandchildren and all who read my memoir to understand both a historical perspective of World War II and what it was like from a child's point of view to grow up in Europe during those years.

KALEVA

Grandmother and I walked up the hill into town to buy milk. I carried the empty milk can. A large woman on the other side of the street saw us and called to my grandmother, "Wait, I am coming over." I amused myself by twirling the milk can around while they chatted. Suddenly I felt the hands of this huge woman grab and shake my shoulders. She had tears in her eyes as she hovered over me: "You poor little girl, losing your mother like that to those awful Russians."

My mother and eight others were the first casualties of World War II in Estonia, which formally began three days later when the Soviet Red Army occupied the country. For some time I did not understand what war was but I was aware that there was something about how she died that made her death memorable to others. I did not even remember my mother. I knew her only from photographs. To me, her death meant that I would never know her.

On June 14, 1940, two days before my second birthday, my mother happened to be a passenger on the *Kaleva*, a Finnish airplane en route from Estonia to Finland. Just minutes into the flight two Soviet Naval Air Force planes approached and fired their machine guns. *Kaleva* was hit and plunged into the Gulf of Finland. My mother was 24 years old and on her way to her father's funeral.

On this fateful day my mother was grieving two deep losses. Two days before, the shrill sound of the telephone had awakened her. The switchboard operator had said, "I have a call for you from Finland." It could not be good news, since long distance calls were expensive and made infrequently. On the other end she heard soft crying. She could tell it was her mother. My mother's beloved father had died at four that morning. She was aware that he had been ill but she had not thought that he would die. Now all she could think of was how to get to Finland.

Finnish airliner *Kaleva*

Later that afternoon she decided to walk to her mother-in-law's house, leaving me at home with Solveig, my Finnish babysitter. As she neared the house, situated on top of a hill overlooking Lake Viljandi, she became alarmed. Something was wrong. There were cars in the driveway and she could hear sobbing. My grandfather had gone to work that morning. He often walked to the nearby orchard he owned to eat his lunch. He was found there under an apple tree, having had a massive stroke, and was brought home where he died. The time of death was listed as four in the afternoon. On the same day, 12 hours apart, my parents had each lost their fathers.

Gunvor Maria Luts

By origin my mother was Finnish—of Swedish descent—but she became Estonian by marrying an Estonian, and she was always referred to as the only Estonian to have been killed on the *Kaleva*.

Recently, simply out of curiosity, I went online and searched for my mother's name, Gunvor Maria Luts. It was eerie to have her name pop up immediately with various links. I clicked on the Wikipedia link and was taken aback to see a black-and-white photo that I did not know existed. It was a photo of a few passengers walking across the tarmac toward an airplane. In the lead was a woman wearing a hat and a suit. I felt goose bumps on my arms when I examined this photo. Several men sporting hats follow her, coats flung over their arms and briefcases in hand. In large letters on the plane was written OH-ALL, signifying that this was a Finnish airplane and, in smaller letters near the door, was the name KALEVA. Near the *Kaleva* sat another plane, about the same size, with a swastika emblazoned on its tail. Although the Finns had been using the swastika symbol for many years before it became associated with the Nazis in Germany, this appeared to be a German plane. A few minutes after two in the afternoon, *Kaleva*, following its regular schedule, began its flight.

The text with the photo stated: "The aircraft was shot down by two Soviet Ilyushin DB-3 bombers on June 14, 1940, while en route from Tallinn to Helsinki ... The bombers opened fire with their machine guns and badly damaged *Kaleva*, making it crash into the water a few kilometers northeast of Keri lighthouse. All nine passengers and crew members on board were killed." Was it possible that this lone woman about to enter the airplane was my mother? If someone had truly captured a photo of that flight, then this had to be my mother. She was the only woman on board.

I had mixed reactions to seeing the photo. For one, it gave me a last glimpse of my mother. Yet I also shivered knowing that she was about to enter what became an inferno, just minutes after takeoff.

Sometime later I saw that beneath the photo was a small caption, "*Kaleva* at the Malmi Airport in the late 1930s," meaning that the photo was taken in Helsinki, not Tallinn. I was disappointed, but that information explained a discrepancy that had puzzled me. When I met Solveig in Finland many years later she told me that my mother had stopped by her room before leaving. She had on a black dress and a necklace with a gold cross and said what at the time seemed strange to Solveig: "Remember, Solveig, if anything were to happen to me, I want you to remain with Kristi." The woman in the photo does not have on a black dress. Yet I do cherish the photo, because it allows me to imagine a last glimpse of my mother entering the airplane.

On the *Kaleva*, a Junkers 52 civilian plane belonging to the Finnish carrier Aero O/Y, were the Finnish pilot and copilot and seven passengers. The passengers included two Germans, two French citizens, one Swede, one American, and my mother, listed as Estonian. All supposedly were diplomats connected with their embassies with the exception of one businessman and my mother.

There has been a lot of speculation why the Soviets shot down the *Kaleva*. One theory holds that the French diplomatic couriers and Henry W. Antheil Jr., the American diplomatic courier with the Helsinki legation, were removing from their respective embassies sensitive material that the Russians wanted to intercept. Other speculations were that the plane was taking the Estonian President into exile or that Estonian gold was being carried to the West. Then there is a simpler explanation: the Russians wanted to provoke Estonia and to close its borders to keep people from leaving the country. In that the Russians succeeded, and three days later the Red Army occupied Estonia. From that point on Estonia was no longer an independent country and was officially declared a satellite of the Soviet Union.

Several small Estonian fishing boats were in the vicinity of Keri Island and the fishermen saw *Kaleva* plunge into the water. They were the first to salvage debris as it rose to the surface, retrieving pieces of the plane, clothes, portfolios, mail pouches, and loose items that had belonged to the passengers. Suddenly a Soviet submarine surfaced. The sailors on the submarine threatened the fishermen and demanded that they hand over everything they had gathered. The fishermen later reported that among sundry items there were two diplomatic pouches, which may have belonged to the American and French diplomats.

Not until 50 years later, when Estonia had regained its independence from the Soviet Union, did it become possible to investigate why the *Kaleva* was attacked. Until then, the Soviet Union had sealed access to all information pertaining to the *Kaleva*.

In 1993, Finn Air erected a memorial to the victims on Keri Island. This was a cooperative effort between Finland and Estonia, because the *Kaleva* was a Finnish plane and Keri Island belongs to Estonia. I was thrilled when I heard the news, since now my mother and all who perished on the *Kaleva* were memorialized as victims of Soviet aggression. I knew in my heart that one day I would take a trip to Keri Island.

In 2005 Ants Vist, an Estonian film producer, and Toivo Kallas, an architect and researcher, began work on a documentary called *The Mystery of the Kaleva*. Their aim was to search for the wreckage of the *Kaleva*, bring it to land, and obtain definitive answers to questions about why the Soviets targeted the *Kaleva*. There were six different search attempts in all. The last one, with the help of the United Sates Navy oceanographic survey ship *Pathfinder,* used sophisticated sonar equipment, but found nothing.

The documentary they produced includes interviews with relatives of the *Kaleva's* passengers and crew whom the producer was able to locate after all these years. Ants Vist interviewed me at my home in Annapolis, Maryland, where I talked about my mother and why she was going to Finland.

Even with all this effort the mystery remains, but there are still people in Estonia interested in finding the plane. There has been speculation that the Soviets recovered the plane, but there is no evidence to support that theory. What we know for certain is that neither the Estonian president nor Estonian gold were on the *Kaleva.*

In the summer of 2013 I was in Estonia on the seventy-third anniversary of the *Kaleva* tragedy. I was excited to find out that the documentary *The Mystery of the Kaleva* was being shown on Estonian television. For me it was a very special evening to be able to watch the documentary in Estonia at the home of relatives.

Through the years I had heard various stories about how my mother happened to be on this particular airplane. When I was eleven years old I visited my aunt in Sweden, traveling there from Austria with my grandmother. There I met Grandmother's friend from Estonia, now living in Sweden, who told me that she probably was the last person to speak with my mother. She worked at a coffee shop and my mother had stopped by. According to her, my mother had been so relieved to meet someone she knew and with whom she could talk, she had apparently decided to take a later flight instead of the one she originally planned to take. I had heard earlier that my mother might have been late arriving at the airport and therefore missed her original flight.

Henry W. Antheil Jr.

Many years later, I heard that my mother could have had another reason to change her flight. She knew Henry W. Antheil Jr., a diplomatic courier for the U.S. State Department who was booked on this later flight. He was carrying coding equipment and other sensitive material from the U.S. legations in Moscow and Tallinn to Finland. This was potentially the last opportunity to remove sensitive materials from the embassies since a Soviet blockade seemed imminent. It is possible that my mother changed her reservation in order to visit with Antheil. He was engaged to a woman named Greta who was the same age as my mother and was also from my mother's hometown, Grankulla, Finland. Henry Antheil and my mother may have been delighted to meet by chance at the Tallinn airport.

In 2007, I was invited to a U.S. State Department Foreign Service Memorial Ceremony in Washington, D.C., when Henry Antheil's name was finally, after 67 years, added to the plaque "honoring those who had paid the ultimate sacrifice while serving their country abroad in the line of duty."

On the world stage, the Soviet attack on the *Kaleva* was overshadowed by the German invasion of Paris on the same day, June 14, 1940. The Soviet Red Army was poised to occupy Estonia and succeeded in doing so on the 17th of June. With that act, Estonia's independence of 22 years, flanked by two world wars, was over. The *Kaleva* was the last plane to fly out of the Tallinn airport to Helsinki; air traffic between the two cities did not resume until March 1990.

When I was about nine years old my grandmother told me a story that frightened me greatly. Some days after the *Kaleva* was shot down a man who read tarot cards approached her on the street in Viljandi and claimed that my mother had come to see him a few weeks earlier. He had not liked what he saw when he spread out the cards. The way he read the cards, there was something about water that concerned him. He said he had told her to stay away from water. When he heard that my mother had perished on the *Kaleva* he said that he was certain that was what he had seen.

For a while I had nightmares about the tarot card reader. I saw my mother sitting on a soft high-backed chair, with a table before her, in a room dimly lit and with the curtains drawn. Before her sat a small, slender man, dressed in black, and eager to read the cards. He took out a deck of cards, shuffled them and carefully laid them out. He gazed at the cards before him and shivered. He did not like what he saw. He gathered up the cards and spread them out again. He did that three times. Each time the result was the same. My mother was no longer looking at the cards, but at him. I could see his body begin to grow so that he loomed over her as he warned her, "I see something about water. Stay away from water!"

At that moment I would wake up, relieved that it was only a dream. I never saw my mother's reaction to this warning. I was certain I would never go to a fortune teller nor want to hear what they said to people who went to them. I feared that indeed they could see the future. After all, this tarot card reader had seen what was going to happen to my mother. I remember wondering, would my mother still be alive if she had not gone to see him or if she had followed his advice? My grandmother believed in superstitions and that fortune tellers could see the future.

At the time the *Kaleva* was shot down, Finland decided not to compromise its fragile political situation with the Union of Soviet Socialist Republics (USSR). Finland had just succeeded in pushing back the invading Red Army in what became known as the Winter War and thus had retained its independence. A possible resumption of war might have been costly to Finland.

Apparently Estonian and Finnish newspapers and radio made minimal mention of the assault on the *Kaleva*. Instead, the media reported that the *Kaleva* exploded and plunged into the Gulf of Finland. Officially the Soviet shooting down of the *Kaleva* never happened; the loss was an accident of undetermined cause. The wives of the Finnish pilot, Bo von Willebrand, and copilot, Tauno Launis, were informed that a Soviet plane had shot down the *Kaleva,* but they were told they could not talk about what they knew and had to sign a promise of secrecy.

The downing of the *Kaleva* was followed a few days later by the Soviet invasion. The Russian Bear had sunk its claws into Estonia and my life became a frantic escape from its reach.

MY HOMELAND, ESTONIA

I think of myself as Estonian-American, having lived in the United States since 1952. Estonia, where I spent five of my first six years, is situated in northern Europe. To the east lies Russia and directly north, separated by 53 miles of water, lies Finland. Estonia, Latvia, and Lithuania are referred to as the three Baltic countries, yet Estonians identify themselves more with the Finns. The Estonian and Finnish languages are similar, both belonging to the Finno-Ugric language family, while those of Latvia and Lithuania belong to the Balto-Slavic language family. Over the centuries, Denmark, Germany, Sweden, and Russia have all ruled Estonia. Not until after World War I, on February 24, 1918, did Estonia gain its independence. This small country, with more than a million people and a long history of being governed by other nations, finally took charge of its own future.

When I was born on June 16, 1938, Estonia was a parliamentary democracy. On the world stage, Hitler had been elected chancellor of Germany in 1933 and, shortly thereafter, assumed dictatorial powers, declaring the Nazi party the only political party in Germany. The Soviet Union—in our home always referred to as Russia or the Red Bear—had become a communist country led by the savage dictator Joseph Stalin. The European economies were still struggling to come out of a devastating economic depression.

Although turmoil was brewing in the world, life in Estonia for my parents was relatively comfortable. My father, Hans Luts, was a director in the family lumber business in Viljandi, a town of about 10,000 people near the center of Estonia. My father's sister Liidi spent several weeks one summer as an exchange student in Finland, where she lived with my mother's family. Later she invited my mother, then Gunvor Maria Ek, to Estonia. During the course of several visits, she and my father fell in love and married in 1936. When they were expecting me, my mother went for three weeks to Helsinki to give birth. She wanted to be with her family and it was important to her that I be born in Finland.

Estonia and Europe in 1939

My parents had settled in Viljandi. They lived briefly with my grandparents, Linda and Juhan Luts, in the big white house that my grandfather had built overlooking Lake Viljandi, but my mother preferred a place of their own. My Aunt Helga (my father's sister) and Uncle Werner and their two children, Hans and Taimi, were comfortable living there.

In those days, having several generations live together, especially if the house was large, was not at all unusual.

With my parents, Gunvor and Hans Luts

At the time when my mother had taken the fateful trip on *Kaleva* to Helsinki, major changes had occurred in Europe, the most significant being that World War II had begun.

Estonia, however, still cherished its independence. The way I understood it—as a young child—Hitler and Stalin had agreed to sell Estonia to Russia. I now know that this notion referred to the Molotov-Ribbentrop secret non-aggression treaty, also known as the Hitler-Stalin Pact, which Germany and the USSR signed on August 23, 1939. These two totalitarian powers connived to divide Europe into "spheres of influence," agreeing that each country was free to occupy designated areas without fear of retaliation by the other. The three Baltic countries, Finland, part of Romania, and the eastern part of Poland were all in the Russian "sphere."

1939 - Germany and the USSR divide up Eastern Europe. The Baltic States fall
under Soviet control and Poland is cut down the middle.[1]

For Estonia, this meant that the Soviet Union was intent
on reclaiming Estonia. For more than 200 years before gaining
independence, Estonia had been part of the Russian Empire,
ruled by the Tsar. On September 1, 1939, the "Wehrmacht"—
the German army created by Hitler in 1935—invaded Poland
from the west, and two weeks later the Soviet Red Army in-

---

[1] This map shows the actual division of Eastern Europe between Germany and
the USSR. The original pact had Lithuania in the German "sphere of influence"
and a part of Romania was to go to the USSR.

vaded Poland from the east. Hitler and Stalin had secretly planned both assaults. Poland had mutual assistance treaties with both England and France, and the invasion of Poland marked the beginning of World War II in Europe as both England and France declared war on Germany.

The Red Army marches into Estonia, ending 20 years of independence.

Estonia, at the outbreak of World War II, remained a neutral country. The Soviet Union, however, began moving its military forces to the Estonian border. The leaders of the USSR coerced Estonia into a so-called "cooperation agreement" that permitted the USSR to establish military bases in Estonia. (Lithuania and Latvia were subjected to the same "cooperation.") Finland refused to sign such a treaty, with the result that the USSR declared war on Finland. This was known as the Winter War (1939–1940) during which the Finns held back the Soviet Red Army. (A year later the war resumed and eventually a peace accord was reached, with Finland losing a significant part of the country to the USSR.)

The Soviets set up both naval and air bases throughout Estonia and 160,000 troops entered the country with little opposition. On June 16, 1940, the Red Army in Estonia fanned out and occupied the cities, supported by another 90,000 troops coming across the border. On June 21, 1940, the invasion was complete and the communists took control of the government.

RUSSIAN OCCUPATION

The death of my mother and the subsequent Russian invasion of Estonia changed the trajectory of my life. Solveig stayed to care for me after my mother's death. As the political situation in Estonia became more volatile, my father urged her to return to Finland. Commercial travel had been cut off, and she managed to escape on a small fishing boat in the middle of the night and made it safely back to Finland.

The Soviets moved in ruthlessly, quickly taking over the country. Their aim was to rapidly integrate Estonia into the Soviet Union and destroy any semblance of free Estonia. They immediately cut Estonia off from the rest of the world, no longer permitting travel to the West or access to foreign news. The practice of religion was forbidden. They brought in masses of soldiers and tanks and incorporated the Estonian armed forces into the Red Army. They succeeded in creating a state of fear by arresting, executing, or deporting anyone they considered to be elite or opposed to the communists. The Russian Bear was determined to destroy all signs of free enterprise and individual freedoms in order to transform Estonia into a communist country.

The Estonian flag, with its blue, black, and white stripes, could no longer be flown and was replaced by the flag of the USSR, with the yellow hammer and sickle on a red background.

Barely a week after occupying Estonia, the new rulers arranged a demonstration by the workers to show that the people themselves asked for a new government. My father was ordered to close the lumber mill for the day so that the workers could march into town carrying red flags and placards demanding bread and work. The Estonian president was forced to appoint a new government, and the hitherto forbidden Estonian Communist Party resurfaced and succeeded in rigging the elections.

As I have learned about the history of that time, I have been amazed how rapidly its new occupiers took over Estonia. One of the first acts of the new communist parliament was to request that the USSR accept Estonia as a member state. This was not what the majority of Estonians wanted, but their voices were silenced. The former Estonian president, Konstantin Päts, and the chief of the army, Johan Laidoner, were deported to Siberia, and all representatives of foreign countries were asked to leave. The United States and Great Britain did not accept the Russian takeover and kept their legations open.

The communist government issued harsh new directives. My father was fired as director of the family lumber business on the grounds that he was a capitalist. He was appalled when his position was taken over by a communist who had been a shoemaker. Instead of enjoying free enterprise, the country was now run by communists under direction from Moscow. Banks and industries were nationalized. My father and my uncle, both successful businessmen, lived in constant fear of deportation to Siberia, or of execution.

The order that affected our lives the most was the allocation of living space limited to nine square meters per person. The new communist administration divided up Grandmother's large house. My father and I moved in along with a friend of the family and her two sons. A Russian officer with his wife and two children and a Russian captain also were assigned to live with us. The house had only one kitchen that we all had to share.

Estonians were on edge. My father, whom I called "Isa"— Estonian for father—had been in the Estonian National Guard. He knew that the communists were looking for him and that it was only a matter of time before someone would turn him in. There were only a few friends whom he could trust. The atmosphere throughout Estonia was one of suspicion. Where previously there had been trust among people, now everyone became suspect.

Isa had begun to spend less time at home in order to reduce the risk of being arrested. One evening when he was home there were heavy footsteps in the hallway, then a knock, and Uncle Arnold, my godfather, entered with loud hellos. Then his voice changed to a whisper as he said that he came to warn my father. The information was from an Estonian woman who was working for the communists. She had seen my father's name on a list of the next group of people to be rounded up. Uncle Arnold said that she was loyal to the Estonians and that she could be trusted. She had secretly been passing on information that saved her countrymen. When Isa heard that the communists were zeroing in on him, he knew he had to go into hiding immediately. He left that night and made his way to Tallinn, where various friends sheltered him, never too long at any one place. Occasionally he would come to see us, unannounced, only to quickly disappear.

I stayed at the big house in Viljandi with my grandmother, aunt and uncle, and my cousins, Hans and Taimi. We children were annoyed with the two Russian girls who had moved into our house. They were a little older and kept taking our toys and refusing to give them back. My grandmother's house had become a boarding house. The Russian captain was very demanding and expected preferential treatment for himself and his family. The Estonians in the house knew they had to be careful not to say anything negative in case they were overheard by the Russians, who might denounce them to the authorities. Any conversation about getting out of Estonia could only be whispered in the privacy of the bedroom.

Grandmother's house in Viljandi

It was a brutally cold winter. I heard many years later that my father had seriously contemplated putting me on his back and walking across the frozen sea to Finland, a risky crossing apparently attempted by others. That did not seem like a safe plan, so my father and his sister and her husband devised a new plan. My aunt and uncle, Taimi and Hans's parents, would legally adopt me. By giving me their last name, Toffer, I could stay with my cousins and their family in case it became necessary to leave Estonia suddenly or if anything happened to my father. I began to call my cousins' parents "Mutti" and "Pappa," just as my cousins did. I continued to refer to my father as "Isa," while Taimi and Hans called him "Uncle Hans."

Recently I visited Taimi at her home in Chapel Hill, North Carolina, and we went through family papers. That was when I actually saw the adoption papers for the first time. Although I knew I was adopted, I did not know that my adoption became official December 16, 1940, six months after my mother died. I had assumed that it happened several years later. I was always told that the arrangement was such that, after the war ended, my father could legally get me back as his daughter.

Hans and Taimi, my new siblings, and me

Estonians lived in fear, wondering, "When will the knock be on our door?" It had happened to many families already. People just vanished. This was an incredibly stressful time. Pappa lost a lot of weight worrying about what to do. Nighttime was the worst in every home because that's when the secret police generally came for people.

And then Pappa received a letter telling him he had to report to the secret police. He was given a designated time to show up, but no explanation as to why he was being called in. Mutti feared that he might not come back.

When Pappa appeared before the two interrogators, they were rather solicitous and praised him. He wondered what they wanted from him. Soon it became clear: they were offering him a paid job to become an informer for the Soviets. He did not have to think long. He declined. He was told that he was making a mistake and that he should take time to think about it. Over the next couple of weeks he was called in twice more, each time being put under increased pressure.

A rumor was circulating that Hitler was giving Baltic Germans a second chance to return to the "Vaterland"—the fatherland. Mutti whispered to Pappa, "What do you think? Maybe we could try to get out as Baltic Germans?" Pappa replied, shaking his head, "I don't see how we would ever qualify." Hitler's first appeal to the Baltic Germans to return home had been issued shortly after the Molotov-Ribbentrop Agreement went into effect.

Baltic Germans had a long history of living in Estonia, with some families dating as far back as 600 years. Many had high-ranking positions in the Russian Empire (which was dissolved in 1917) and were represented among the royalty. They owned land and manor houses and held important professional positions. Many Baltic Germans recognized the danger of staying in what would surely be a war zone if Germany and the USSR ever went to war. They heeded Hitler's call to return, even though they might not have had contact with Germany for generations. Others chose to remain in Estonia.

As the fear of getting arrested loomed over them, Mutti and Pappa decided to try the Baltic-German route of escape. They had not succeeded in their attempts to obtain permission to enter Finland or Sweden. This second resettlement call to Baltic Germans to return to the German Reich became the last ray of hope for my family, now desperate to escape their likely fate under the Soviet occupation.

In order to be considered Baltic Germans, however, they had to demonstrate that they spoke German and to show some documentation written in German. Pappa had received his textile engineering degree in Leipzig, Germany. Mutti also spoke fluent German, having had a German governess and having studied German in school.

With great trepidation they traveled to Pärnu, a lovely seaport town. They brought various papers with them, including Pappa's university diploma. There were other people in the waiting area. Then it was their turn to appear before the commission, which consisted of one Soviet and one German officer. These two had the power to decide the life or death of the people before them.

The German officer looked at the papers and nodded positively, passing the documentation over to the Soviet officer. He took a quick glance, making it evident that he did not understand the language, shook his head and loudly said, "*Nyet.*" Mutti and Pappa's anxiety rose with every *nyet*, fearing that their last chance to escape was disappearing. Then the German showed the Russian Pappa's mother's confirmation certificate. It was an elaborate document adorned with pictures of angels and palm branches with elaborate German writing. Although her confirmation had taken place in Estonia, the certificate had been printed in Leipzig, Germany. At the time this document was printed it was common practice for Estonians to have special certificates printed in Germany. It certainly didn't mean that the family had German roots. This document somehow convinced the Soviet officer and he gave permission for our whole family, including Grandmother, to leave the country.

Pappa and our family were now officially declared to be Baltic Germans and eligible to return to Germany. For an Estonian to be declared a Baltic German provoked mixed feelings. Many Estonians felt animosity against the Baltic Germans because they had treated the Estonians as serfs. The Baltic German "nobility" looked down at Estonians and refused to learn Estonian. My grandfather, Juhan Luts, had worked as a serf for a landowner at a manor house when he was a teenager. He had declared as a young man that he was just as good as the Germans. He was an enterprising, successful businessman who became wealthy and actually bought a manor house to be used by his family during the summer. I think that he would have approved of his family's "conversion" to Baltic Germans since it was a chance for his grandchildren to survive.

The overwhelming fear of the adults was that we would not get out of Estonia. The border crossings could be closed at any time.

There was a feeling of finality to the travel preparations. Warnings circulated that the secret police would try anything to keep people from leaving. There were constant reports of kidnappings, arrests, and harassment. The Russian captain who lived in our house insisted, when he realized that we were in the process of leaving, that had he known about our plans, he would have prevented our departure. Since we had the official approval of the government of the Soviet Union, he was too late to stop us.

On March 6, 1941, we left Viljandi on a train to Tallinn, where we boarded another train to Germany filled with refugees, just like us, fleeing our homeland. When people spoke it was in whispers:

"Do you think we will get safely across the border?"

"We have our papers."

"That is not going to do us any good."

"You can't trust them. They will detour the train."

Grandmother was convinced that this was the last time she would ever be in Estonia. Mutti and Pappa had been walking the tightrope between arrest and escape for months. We were getting close to succeeding in our escape, but until we crossed the border, we could not feel safe. Everyone feared that they, or their loved ones, would be detained and taken off the train at any point. A soft voice began to sing the Estonian national anthem: "Mu isamaa, mu önn ja rõõm" (My fatherland, my happiness and joy). Spontaneously all joined in with their voices rising in their pride of being Estonians. The mood lifted. They were strong, they would make it.

The Soviet secret police, the NKVD, kept coming around reviewing the documents. One passenger in the next compartment was forcibly removed from the train, alarming all on board. Pappa was convinced that he had spotted on the train the man who had interrogated him several times and urged him to become a traitor. At the border there was a last check of documents, this time by the German police, followed by a hearty, "Welcome to Germany." The relief to have escaped from the clutches of the Russian Bear was immense; however, it was tempered by the anxiety of not knowing what lay ahead for us in Germany.

LIVING IN GERMANY

I don't know how we ended up in Neresheim, a small town in southern Germany. In all likelihood we were assigned there. The whole town came out to welcome us, the returning Baltic Germans, to our "Vaterland." Our new home was an ancient monastery, high on a hill above the town. It was a huge square building built around a courtyard that was being used as a refugee camp. Taimi and I were assigned to sleep in a communal nursery, which upset us terribly. We did not want to be separated from our family and it was only after Hans was permitted to join us that we settled down. Our meals were served in a large dining room, and we children all had to attend nursery school all day long. The three of us had not been in any type of school setting before and initially had a hard time adjusting to the new routine.

Grandmother was distraught to see us so unhappy and insisted that her work assignment be with the nursery-age children. She was fiercely protective of us and succeeded in being able to work where we were. Mutti was assigned to the kitchen, and Pappa got a job working on the railroad. Later Pappa found work in Augsburg in the textile business and he began to look for an apartment so that we could join him, though that never happened. A few months after our arrival in Neresheim Isa also was approved as a Baltic German. His hope was to be near us and to find a job.

I have only one memory of Neresheim. It is the earliest memory that I can recall. We are in a meadow filled with colorful flowers. In the distance is our new home, the monastery of Neresheim. It is a beautiful warm, sunny day. Taimi and I pick daisies and hand them to Mutti, who expertly weaves our flowers into two lovely wreaths. We place them on our heads and jump around in delight. Hans suddenly cries out: Look at the big bird! I look up, and above me circles a huge bird, which might have been a hawk. I am awed by its size and the chance to see one close up. It keeps circling, making wide loops, as if putting on a show for us. Hans, my big five-year-old brother, rather calmly states: "I have heard that these big birds suddenly swoop down and grab little kids." That had not occurred to me, and suddenly I am frightened. At that moment I envision that the bird will stop circling, swoop down, and grab me. I see myself lifted up and carried away in his talons. I run to my grandmother, hold her hand, and no longer can enjoy watching this majestic bird.

Neresheim, Germany

Three months after our arrival in Neresheim, Germany declared war on the USSR. Hitler had double-crossed Stalin and was no longer abiding by the 1939 non-aggression treaty. Our family was overjoyed to get the news that Germany was pushing north through the Baltic countries. The dream of returning to Estonia, which my family had tried to bury, resurfaced. We had come here as Baltic Germans, but we were Estonians eager to return home. Our travels now were dependent on permission from the German government.

1941 - Hitler double-crossed Stalin and attacked the Soviets across a broad front in Eastern Europe.

Isa and other Estonians were eager to join the German army to help push the Red Army back. He wanted to avenge the death of his wife, my mother. He was assigned to the SS[2]

---

[2] The SS, Schutzstaffel, or "protection squadron." Most non-Germans fighting with the German army were assigned to SS units because German law forbade anyone but ethnic Germans from fighting in the regular army, the Wehrmacht.

as a second lieutenant and hoped he would be sent to the Eastern Front where could help free Estonia from the "red plague," a common phrase for communism. Instead he was assigned to a unit in Kiev, in the Ukraine, where he stayed for a year. While we lived in Germany, our news was German news broadcasting Hitler's successes. The daily radio reports were of the swift victories that the German army experienced as it pushed the Soviets out of the Baltic countries. Then the reports came that the Germans had freed Viljandi, then Tartu, and reached Tallinn in August 1941. The Estonian units arrived first and hoisted the blue, black, and white flag to the top of the Pikk Hermann tower next to the Parliament Building. Estonians were jubilant that they had their country back. It soon became apparent, however, that Germany had no intention of supporting Estonia's independence. They were the conquerors and were claiming the Baltic countries for themselves. The Estonian flag that had flown for one day on Pikk Herman was replaced the following day by the German flag sporting the swastika.

With my father in Germany

Estonia was now occupied by Germany. After Germany invaded the USSR, Stalin joined forces with England and France and changed Soviet allegiance from the Axis (Germany, Hungary, Italy, Japan, Romania, and Bulgaria) and joined the Allies (primarily Great Britain and France). Hitler and Stalin were now each methodically and brutally expanding their reach throughout Europe. While the Soviet Union plotted to expand communism, Germany schemed to create a vast Aryan society.

After we had been at the Neresheim monastery for more than seven months, we and all the other people who had found refuge there were urgently reassigned to Heilbronn, a small town in the southern part of Germany. We may have been transferred there as evacuees since this was still an area untouched by air raids, which were becoming more frequent in Neresheim. The people in Heilbronn were not happy that we had been sent into their town.

Summer in Neresheim - Taimi, Hans and me.

Our family had to decide whether to stay in Germany as Baltic Germans or renounce our new classification and return to Estonia. The pull to return to our homeland was very strong. This question was resolved when the German-run government in Estonia requested that Pappa return to Viljandi to restart the former linen factory, where he had been a manager until the Soviets nationalized the business in 1940. He agreed to return and went back to Estonia in June 1942.

The rest of us followed a month later by train. I can still see myself strapped into the overhead baggage compartment (made of rope netting) and looking out the window. I am on my side and have a clear view of the fields, trees, and occasional houses that quickly disappear only to be replaced by new scenes. I enjoy the soothing, rhythmic movement of the train while watching the countryside fly by.

ESTONIA UNDER GERMAN OCCUPATION

O ur return trip to Viljandi took eight days. I was now four years old, and after having been away for more than a year, everything seemed new to me. We were able to stay in our family home overlooking Lake Viljandi, while continuing to share the house with other Estonian families. The Russians, who had lived with us during the Russian occupation, had departed. Pappa had successfully restarted the linen factory. We children immediately felt at home. We again had our playhouse, the big garden, and lots of people around who cared for us.

Grandmother's house had many people living in it who were not known to us. Strangers occupied the rooms that had been assigned to us before we left for Germany. Since Grandmother was the original owner she had a right to occupancy. Family and friends were happy to see us but the strangers in the house resented our return. Other housing had to be found for the people who had been living in our rooms. After several weeks we were able to move back into our quarters. Hans, Taimi, and I shared what was referred to as the children's room. It was a big room and had a beautiful view onto Lake Viljandi. It must be this early fond memory of the lake that has drawn me repeatedly to living by the water.

During the time we spent in Germany it became known that Hitler intended to expand Germany's "Lebensraum"—living space—by taking over as many countries as possible. Owning Estonia was part of his long-range plan.

For my parents it was shocking to discover the atrocities that had been committed in Estonia under the Soviet occupation during our absence. While in Germany we had received letters from Estonia, but since everyone suspected that their letters were in all likelihood opened and read by the NKVD, they had not dared to be candid about what was really happening in our homeland. Pappa discovered that his sister's husband had been deported or killed, as had been other extended-family members and friends. It seemed as if no family living under Russian occupation had been spared. Many of those forcibly removed most likely ended up in Gulags, the labor camps in Siberia.

The worst episode of deportation happened on June 14, 1941, exactly a year after the *Kaleva* was shot down, while we were safe in Neresheim. In one night, 10,000 people were awakened and loaded onto cattle cars headed to remote Siberia. One of Mutti's cousins who lived in Tartu described that night: "The Russians arbitrarily blocked off streets and removed everyone regardless of age or health. The only reason my family was spared was that we lived on a street that was not selected to be blocked off." She sadly recounted how many of her friends had vanished. Of the 10,000 purged, one third were children.

I have greater recall of events after our return to Estonia. At first, memories are little slivers that became more vivid as I turned four and then five. I have wonderful memories of happy times in our two-story playhouse, running in the spacious garden, and playing on the stone veranda overlooking Lake Viljandi.

Our baby sister, Annika, was born in May 1943, and her christening was on the same day as her godmother's wedding. Both events were held at our home. I had never attended such an elegant celebration. A pastor performed the two ceremonies in what used to be the original vast dining room, at that time used for lodging and storage. Now it was transformed into a magical place with long tables, beautiful china, wineglasses, purple flowers, and candles. We children attended the christening and the wedding ceremonies, but were excluded from the dinner and were sent upstairs. When we heard that people were leaving, Hans, Taimi, and I sneaked down and began to pick up wineglasses and sample what was left. We were drinking wine and joyfully running from table to table. Our laughter attracted Mutti, who quickly escorted us back upstairs. What I remember best is Annika in a fancy, pink christening gown—a family heirloom—and the bride wearing the most beautiful dress I had ever seen. It was a long, purple lace dress with a flaring skirt and puffy sleeves. Valida, the bride, was one of our favorite people. She owned a soda bottling factory, and one of our highlights was to walk to her factory, where she would give us each our own bottle of soda.

At Annika's christening -- Hans, Mutti holding Annika, me, Taimi, Pappa

For us children this was a great place to live. We had a spacious garden that surrounded our big house. There was a greenhouse with a grape arbor, a swimming pool that was now an empty pit, a vegetable garden, apple and pear trees, and bushes with gooseberries and currants. At the end of

Mutti's rock garden was our playhouse, called "Villa Rabarber," after the Estonian word for rhubarb, which grew nearby. Taimi and I spent hours there playing with our dolls. Taimi, who was seven months older than I, had a wonderful imagination and would make up stories and tell me what to do. The second floor of the playhouse was Hans's domain and off limits to us unless we were invited.

Next to the playhouse was a chicken coop. We usually had

a flock of chickens, and many mornings Taimi and I would bring our baskets and walk with Grandmother to gather eggs.

One afternoon I was in the playhouse by myself. I saw Grandmother briskly walk down to the chicken coop. She did not see

Villa Rabarber

me. She opened the gate, took some feed from her pocket, threw it on the ground and was quickly surrounded by several hens. I watched as she reached down and grabbed one of the squawking chickens by its legs. She cradled the hen in one arm and, with her free hand, twisted its neck. The hen fluttered in Grandmother's arm and suddenly went limp. At that moment the thought went through my mind, "She killed the chicken." I felt goose bumps on my arms and legs, but couldn't take my eyes off Grandmother. Matter-of-factly she turned around, closed the gate, and walked back to the house with the dead chicken nestled in her arm. I knew that we ate our chickens, but to see the killing actually done so swiftly and smoothly astonished and scared me. I never told anyone, not even Taimi, what I had seen. Taimi returned and we continued playing with our dolls.

For me life was good, and I had no awareness of what was happening politically. My Isa was still in the service. He would write me letters with drawings and send candy to us children. Mutti would take us swimming at the lake below our house. In the winter we would go sledding and be pushed on the frozen lake on a kick sled. My favorite walk was to the nearby ruins of an old castle where there were many paths to explore. Although much of Europe was engulfed in war, I was blissfully innocent of what was going on.

Playing with the kick sled

ISA — MY FATHER

It was a warm summer afternoon, and I had just turned five. Taimi and I had on matching red smocked dresses with white polka dots. We were both barefoot and were walking down a dirt road that had trees and bushes on either side. The road led to our grandmother's house, where we all lived. Taimi and I were chatting with Isa. He had been able to get leave from his company and made it home a couple of days after my birthday. The three of us had just been in town. We had stopped at the newspaper office, where we visited my godfather, Arnold, who was my father's best friend. Uncle Arnold loved it when we came by and always made us giggle.

Taimi and I skipped ahead of my father. When I glanced back, Isa had disappeared. Both Taimi and I looked around. He had just been here. Where did he go? He had vanished. We couldn't understand it. Suddenly we heard some rustling behind some bushes. Isa jumped up and yelled, "BOO!" We both laughed in surprise and relief to know where he was. A little farther up the road, he disappeared again. This time we knew that he was hiding, and we squealed in delight when he reappeared. He repeated this many times, and I remember that after a while it was no longer fun. As we continued down the road, I stubbed my big toe. A little blood oozed onto the ground, and I burst into tears. Isa quickly reappeared, picked me up, lifted me onto his shoulders, took Taimi's hand, and we headed home.

I have only one other memory of Isa, an event that may have occurred a little earlier. Hans, Taimi, and I were called to the living room. Isa was standing on the other side of the room wearing his soldier uniform. I knew that it was Isa, but at first I was not sure that I recognized him. In his soldier uniform he looked different and very tall. I stared at him trying to compare this man to the father I thought I remembered,

Hans Luts

not having seen him for what seemed like a long time. Then he called to me. I recognized his voice and ran into his arms.

One day it was winter and snowing outside. Hans, Taimi, and I were in the children's room. We played tiddlywinks and then watched by the window as the snowflakes came down. I don't recall what prompted me to run to Grand-mother's room to tell her something. I opened the door, and there was my grandmother lying on her bed, wailing. Mutti stood up with tears running down her face, pulled me toward her and said, "Your Isa has died." If she said anything else, I do not remember it.

What I do recall vividly is that the curtains were closed, which made the room dark, and the loud sobbing, which frightened me. I could not wait to get out of that room. Previously this was one of my favorite rooms of the house. I dashed out of the room and told Taimi and Hans that my Isa had died. I knew that my father's death somehow meant that I would never see him again, just as had happened to my mother. I also had the thought that from now on I was no longer going to have two fathers, which had made me different from Hans and Taimi. That fact had made me feel special, but also set me apart. It had been confusing to have two fathers and have my brother and sister call my Isa "Uncle Hans." I also distinctly remember having a feeling of loss upon hearing of my father's death.

My father died on November 27, 1943, at age 34, while serving as an SS lieutenant in Latvia. He had gone to the University of Tartu and graduated with a degree in business and economics, intending to take over the family businesses. With the outbreak of World War II his life was on a track he no longer controlled. When he first went to Germany in 1941 as a returned Baltic German, Isa intended to find a job. Instead, shortly after his arrival, Germany began its advance into the Baltic countries and Isa enlisted in the German army.

I still have some letters that he wrote to his mother and sisters from the various places where he was stationed. The lack of information about his assignments is striking. Instead, he generally wrote about the weather and being grateful for the packages sent to him from home, especially the delicious apples. That was a delicacy that he could not get. He no doubt knew that every word he was writing most likely would be read by the censor. There is one letter in which he wrote in detail about his first Christmas (1941), which he celebrated with his German division mates as a soldier assigned to Kiev, Ukraine. He described how they decorated a tree with pinecones, flags, and candles. The men cleared one wall so that a big portrait of Adolf Hitler could be hung there. The piano was pushed to the side to leave room for the men to gather. They quietly sang "O Christmas Tree," after which their company leader gave a short speech about how the light of Christmas would guide them to win over darkness. When they sang "Silent Night" the men could no longer look at each other because their eyes were damp; some had to leave the room. The Christmas celebration was followed with wine and beer, some chocolate and sweets, and other treats.

In a letter to my grandmother on January 4, 1942, Isa wrote that the temperature was minus 34 degrees Celsius (minus 29 degrees Fahrenheit). He said that he was thankful that he was able to keep warm because he had received a heavy coat and a hat that covered his ears. The only part of him that was exposed to the cold air was his nose. He had learned to apply petroleum jelly to keep it from freezing. This gave a little glimpse of his duties. He apparently was assigned to a watch post for eight-hour shifts. He was outside for two hours, relieved by another soldier, and then resumed his outdoor watch. After describing the cold, he shifted to writing about how they all longed for spring, which was still two to three months away. He wistfully hoped that they would soon turn back their communist enemy, after which they would all be able to return to their homes and resume the work they had chosen for their professions. This was the closest he came in his letters to sharing his longing to return home and resume a normal life.

After a year in Kiev he was assigned to the Italian Alps where he was happy to be part of an Estonian regiment. He delighted in the beautiful scenery and made a passing comment about receiving training as a translator. Every letter prominently stated on the top that it was written in the Estonian language.

Next he was sent to Latvia where he also was with an Estonian regiment. He was in charge of training young 17- and 18-year-old boys for action at the front. In a letter written a month before he died he said that they would very likely be sent to the front near Peipsi Lake, on the border between Estonia and Russia, to keep the Russians from re-entering Estonia. He sounded excited because his ambition had always been to help keep the communists out of Estonia.

Isa never made it to Lake Peipsi. At the time of his death he was riding a motorcycle on a military assignment and the motorcycle struck a land mine. He was severely wounded in the explosion and died six days later. I have a copy of the letter that his attending physician wrote to my grandmother to tell her about his last days. It is a lengthy letter describing Isa's severe injuries and how they tried everything they could to save him. He let us know that my father would be buried with full military honors in Riga, Latvia. As I read the letter I was touched by the care and concern the doctor conveyed to

Grandmother about the last days of her dear son's life. The closing words of the letter, before signing his name, were "Heil Hitler."

Age 5 in Viljandi

Shortly before Christmas, after my father's death, I received a package put together by an Estonian organization. These packages were for children who had lost a parent fighting for the freedom of Estonia. In the package was a lovely little doll wearing a pretty dress, and candy and chocolate. If there was anything else, I do not recall. I remember happily announcing to all that it would be great to get more packages like that. Grandmother must have been appalled because she said sternly to me, "Don't ever say anything like that again." Only years later did I understand that she must have interpreted what I said to mean that I thought more people should die so I could get another package. Of course I only meant that I was thrilled to get such a pretty doll and the sweets.

THE RUSSIAN BEAR ADVANCES

It was 1944 and the war continued to rage throughout Europe. The Germans had occupied Estonia since June 1941 and we were settled back in our rooms at Grand-mother's house. Even the five crates of furniture we had taken to Germany when we went there as Baltic Germans were returned. During the 15 months we had spent in Germany, they had been safely stored in a warehouse and were never opened.

The Germans did not free Estonia, and it became clear that they had no intention of leaving. Estonians put their hope of regaining their independence after the war in the Atlantic Charter. After all, this is what Winston Churchill, the prime minister of Great Britain, and Franklin D. Roosevelt, president of the United States, had spelled out on August 14, 1941. The Charter declared the Allied goals for a post-war world: freedom of self-determination, economic security, and open trade for all countries. It meant a lot to Estonians to know that there were powerful countries supporting Estonia's right to return to independence at the conclusion of the war.

The Germans, who were happily welcomed by Estonians when they pushed out the occupying Soviet army, were committing their own brutalities. From the Nazi point of view the Estonian economy was primarily there to meet German war needs. In the first year they were in Estonia the Germans arrested close to 19,000 people, many of whom were communists, and executed more than 6,000 of them. Fewer than half of the arrested people were released after interrogation and the rest were sent to concentration camps. The German Nazis ordered the extermination of 923 Estonian Jews and brought in 9,000 Jews from Central and Eastern Europe for extermination. After the war it became known that Hitler had drawn up definitive plans to make Estonia part of the greater German empire.

1944 - The Soviets went on the offensive.

Then it became obvious to everyone that the USSR was preparing to re-enter Estonia. The Russians considered the Baltic countries to be theirs and were determined to reclaim what belonged to them. The assault began in March 1944 with a heavy bombardment of Tallinn. Systematically they pushed into Estonia from different directions. As the fighting came closer to Viljandi, our family decided to rent some rooms in a farmhouse a couple of miles outside of town. Since the fear of air attack was greater at nighttime, our parents felt that we would be safer to sleep in the country. At first we walked there every evening and returned to our home in town the next morning. I recall getting firm warnings that we were not to pick up anything on the way, because something that might look like candy could be a camouflaged explosive. This admonition intrigued me and I began to point out various paper scraps and shiny objects along the road while repeating the question, "Is this an explosive?" "Is this an explosive?"

Walking to the farmhouse outside of town: Taimi, Hans, Kristina, and Mutti, with Annika in the stroller

We enjoyed living on the farm, and after a while, we were able to stay there instead of making the long trek back and forth. Nearby was a brook with lively fish, and over at the barn were cows, chickens, kittens, and dogs. Best of all, there were other kids to play with. I had a playmate by the name of August who enjoyed playing tag and other games with us. He was perhaps a year older than I was and he kept saying that he wanted to marry me. I liked his attention and enjoyed our stay in the country.

One time, as we walked back to Viljandi, I was shocked when I saw our house. I could not believe what I was seeing. Our beautiful family house on Lake Viljandi, referred to by all as "The White House," was now dull gray. I found out that the house had been camouflaged so that it would not be such a visible target to the enemy. This change made it real to me that the Russian Bear was approaching, but I did not yet contemplate what that might mean for us.

The Red Army continued its advance on Estonia and the bombing attacks were getting closer to Viljandi. Pappa and Mutti feared that the USSR would retake Estonia and that we would be at its mercy, just as we had been during the first occupation before leaving for Germany. The thought of living under communism was intolerable to our parents. We joined the exodus of 70,000 people who made the difficult decision to flee before the USSR retook our country. The people who were fleeing all fervently hoped to return to their homeland after the war.

FLEEING ESTONIA

Y ou can each bring one doll," Mutti said to my sister Taimi and me. We were in our playhouse, "Villa Rabarber." We took our dolls from their beds, made their beds, and neatly arranged all our other toys. Our parting words to our toys were: "We will be back soon."

It was 45 years later, in 1989, that I first returned to Estonia. The paint on the sign "Villa Rabarber" was barely legible. The path past Mutti's rock garden to our playhouse was as I remembered it. But much had changed since I was six years old. Grandmother's house was divided into 11 apartments, with each family having an assigned garden plot in which to raise vegetables and flowers. Our house, overlooking Lake Viljandi, was still grey from when it was painted for camouflage. As I looked at it from the lakeside, it was still the largest house around.

In September 1944, we four children, parents, and grandmother were fleeing again from Estonia, this time heading to Austria. I had no real understanding of what it all meant. I could see that the grownups were busy deciding what to take and what to leave behind. I did not understand the apprehension they must have felt knowing that the Red Army was marching ever closer. Mutti and Pappa must have constantly feared that we would not be able to get out of Estonia. To me, initially, this trip seemed like an adventure.

We left our home in Viljandi on an overcrowded train headed for Tallinn. Mutti and Pappa made the rounds to the Finnish and Swedish embassies hoping to get visas so that we could leave Estonia. After standing in line for days on end, they had no success. On September 20, 1944, there was shooting and bombing in Tallinn. The rumor spread that the Russians were approaching and the Germans were departing. Mutti and Pappa decided that we had to go to the harbor early the next morning. Their hope was that we could get out of Estonia on one of the German ships about to depart. My most vivid memory is of what turned out to be our last breakfast in Estonia. We had scrambled eggs and black bread with butter. I recall having the distinct sensation that what I was eating was absolutely delicious. The taste and smell stayed in my consciousness for a long time.

The harbor was filled with people, and for the first time I became aware of the tension in my parents and grandmother. I had never been in such a mass of men, women, and children all loaded down with luggage. I too became anxious to get on a ship and now understood that we had to get away before the Red Bear captured us. A number of big ships were in the harbor. The biggest ship, the *Moero*, had large Red Cross markings. It was transporting wounded German soldiers in addition to German civilians and had room for some Estonian refugees. Next to it was a smaller ship, the *Lapland*. We were in a long line that slowly advanced toward a man in uniform carrying a gun. His job was to assign people to different ships. Much to the disappointment of my parents, we were told to board the *Lapland*. They had wanted to be on the *Moero*, since under conventional rules of war, Red Cross ships carrying wounded soldiers were considered off limits to enemy attack.

In the early evening our ship left the harbor. We had been standing on deck watching the people board. Now we pulled out of the harbor, part of a convoy of five ships. We had barely left when I heard voices calling out in relief and agony, "Tallinn is burning." I could see a red hue and smoke in the area we had just left. I was standing next to Pappa, who handed me his binoculars. I had never looked through binoculars before and could not see anything. He impatiently asked,

"Don't you see it?" My answer was a decided, "No, I can't see a thing." The binoculars felt heavy and awkward in my small hands. After he asked me the third time, I simply said, "Yes," and handed them back. I never saw anything through the binoculars. My eyes saw the redness in the sky and the smoke. Tallinn had been attacked by the Russian Bear. I understood that we had escaped its clutches at the last possible moment. Years later I learned that most of the fires were set by the Germans as their last act before the ships left the harbor. The USSR officially occupied Estonia the next day.

A day later, while Taimi and I were playing on deck, our play was interrupted by the piercing wail of the onboard siren. A loud voice announced that we had to go below deck immediately. We grabbed our toys and headed for the door to our quarters, with Grandmother close behind. There must have been several hundred women and children in our huge room. We ran over to our beds, relieved to find Mutti and baby Annika sitting there. We heard loud booms in succession. Abruptly our ship swerved violently from side to side while continuing to sway. We smelled smoke. People desperately screamed, "We have been hit! We are sinking!" The lights went out. Frantic women, some holding the hands of their children, were rushing toward the open door. I was frightened and felt reassured when Mutti simply said, "We will stay right here until we know what is going on."

A tall burly man wearing a uniform positioned himself in the doorway, the only door to the outside, with his arms blocking the entrance, and bellowed, "No one can leave. Everyone sit down and stay where you are." The room instantaneously became quiet, as if the air had been sucked out of the place. Grandmother crawled into bed, pulled a blanket over her head, and insisted that I stay with her. I went with her but didn't want to stay there and soon wriggled out from under her arms to join Mutti, Taimi, and sixteen-month-old baby Annika. Pappa and Hans were staying in the men's quarters.

We sat there for what seemed like a long time, not knowing what was happening. If we talked at all it was in soft whispers. Some people were crying, but what I remember most was the silence of fear around me. We did not know if our ship had been hit. The lights flickered, went out, returned, and went out again, leaving us in darkness, with the silhouette of the tall man in the doorway, the only place where light came in. Then the power returned, but not as brightly as before. Our ship stopped swaying.

The loudspeaker came on with the announcement that the *Moero*, the Red Cross ship, had been hit and was sinking. I can still see the huge man in the doorway stepping aside and women, their clothes soaking wet, being brought in. Some were on stretchers, some walking and staring with vacant eyes, others sobbing and screaming. I began to understand what had happened: our ship had survived and theirs had sunk. One woman looked at us, Mutti with three girls, and burst into uncontrollable sobs. Her three little girls had been with her on the *Moero*, and she had no idea how they got separated. She feared they had all drowned. I was trembling when I heard that and felt scared with the commotion around me.

This is what I learned later: The Moero, after being hit by Russian aerial torpedoes, sank quickly. Ships in the vicinity rescued only about 450 of the more than 1,100 passengers on board. Most of the wounded German soldiers perished. The people who survived had jumped into the water to escape the burning ship. Our ship, the Lapland, had been traveling in the shadow of the Moero, no doubt because the proximity to a Red Cross ship might give it protection in case of attack. It was never determined if the torpedoes were intended for our ship or if the Russians were blatantly disregarding international law. I grew up feeling certain that what I first heard was the truth: the captain of our ship had made a heroic zigzag maneuver to avoid the torpedoes, thus saving our lives.

When the *Lapland* arrived at the harbor in Danzig, Poland, it was a beautiful, sunny day. Grandmother took us children to a grassy spot near the shore while our parents dealt with the luggage and figured out where we would go next. "Look up, look up. There is a Zeppelin." I lifted my eyes. Above me gently floated a huge dirigible. It was the most awesome sight I had ever seen.

Many years later I learned that Danzig (now Gdansk) was where World War II had started in Europe. It was in Danzig that the German army entered Poland in September 1939. Five years later, in September 1944, we had arrived in Danzig and were headed to Austria. All we had to rely on was a letter from a German soldier, who had befriended our parents when the Germans occupied Estonia, asking his father-in-law in Vöcklabruck, Austria, to give us refuge.

We were among the very last people to flee Estonia. The choice to leave for our family was based on hope for survival, just as it had been in 1941, when we fled to Germany as Baltic Germans. Staying in Estonia would have meant either deportation to Siberia or possible death for our parents because they were educated and capitalists. They took the chance that fleeing to Austria by way of Poland and Germany was the wisest choice.

Now all seven of us—four children, parents, and our grandmother—were headed by train through Poland and Germany. We squeezed into a cattle car with other refugees. German soldiers of various nationalities were already on board, being transferred to a new front. The soldiers kindly let us children sleep on the hay that had been thrown on the floor and shared treats with us. We were on our way to Austria where we would be safe from the claws of the Russian Bear.

DESTINATION: AUSTRIA

Most refugees who left Estonia in 1944 had no idea where they would end up. Our family had a destination: Vöcklabruck, Upper Austria. In his coat pocket, Pappa carried a letter given to him by the German soldier, Mr. Mayerhofer. The letter was addressed to his father-in-law, Mr. Czerwenka.

Mr. Mayerhofer had come to Estonia with his German regiment. He had been wounded in Estonia, met some good friends of my parents, and had been a frequent guest at our home in Estonia. In gratitude, he wrote a letter to his father-in-law asking him to help us if we ever had to leave Estonia. We took a chance by trusting this soldier's belief that indeed his father-in-law would welcome us.

After many days of travel, we arrived tired and dirty in Vöcklabruck, a beautiful medieval town at the edge of the Alps. We stayed outside the train station, sitting on our luggage, while Pappa went to find Mr. Czerwenka. I could hear the tension in Grandmother's voice. "What will we do if they don't help us? Where will we go?" Mutti in her typical way said, "We will figure that out when we have to." Her practical attitude to not create extra problems helped us deal with the uncertain world we found ourselves in. We learned from her to accept life as it was and to make the best of it.

After what seemed like a very long time, Pappa, accompanied by Mrs. Mayerhofer pushing a wheelbarrow, came to get us. Pappa had given Mr. Czerwenka the precious letter on which hinged our hopes for refuge. After Mr. Czerwenka had shared the letter with his wife and daughter, they graciously welcomed us. As we trudged down the street with Pappa pushing the wheelbarrow with our luggage, I saw a big yellow villa with a turret set back from the road surrounded by a garden behind a wrought-iron fence. Mrs. Mayerhofer stopped at the ornate gate: "We are here."

The Czerwenkas' House in Vöcklabruck

Two girls and a boy around our ages came running to welcome us. The first thing we did was to bathe, which we had not done since leaving Estonia a week earlier. This was followed by a meal. I don't remember what we ate, but I do recall that we sat at a huge table and were served by the kitchen help. Mr. Czerwenka's three grandchildren were staying with their grandparents, so we immediately had playmates. The girls first showed Taimi and me their dolls, and then we played under the tall trees in the garden. Mutti was in a lot of pain from a fall she had taken on our ship during the chaos of the Russian attack that sank the *Moero*. She had received no medical care, and her knee had become badly infected. On our second day in Vöcklabruck, she was admitted to the hospital. She was a patient there for several weeks, while the doctors successfully fought the virulent infection and saved her leg.

Mr. Czerwenka was an influential man in Vöcklabruck. He was a well-to-do businessman with the Eternit Company, makers of roof tiles, and the biggest employer in town. He arranged lodging for us at his sister's house, which was near one of the two large medieval towers in the center of Vöcklabruck, a couple of blocks from his villa. The street she lived on had originally been a moat back in the 15th century.

Vöcklabruck, Austria

Her house had two stories, a dirt-floor cellar, and a small enclosed porch. The main-level windows on the street side had curved wrought-iron bars about eight inches apart across the lengths of the windows. I had never seen anything like that before. Our family had a kitchen and one big room on the main level. Across the street was a park with benches and shade trees. Grandmother and I shared a bed and slept in the kitchen. The five others shared the big room. In the winter that room was very cold, and on many mornings, the windows as well as the interior walls near the windows were covered with ice. There may have been a small woodstove in a corner of the room, but I do not recall if we were able to use it. Firewood and coal were hard to get, and the little we had was used for cooking and to keep some warmth in the kitchen.

I was scared of the man next door. He seemed old and not very tall, with uncombed hair, and he wore the same stained shirt day after day. I do not know if he had any other clothes since whenever I saw him he looked the same. He would shuffle around his yard, usually accompanied by his big brown dog. Our kitchen window, this one without wrought-iron bars, faced his yard. His wife wore long, stained dresses and smelled of urine. When I commented on the smell, Mutti explained that when women get older, sometimes they can no longer hold their urine. I was appalled by the fate that could be awaiting me.

One night I woke up to go to the bathroom. As I passed the window I saw the neighbor man with a shotgun over his shoulder, pacing back and forth before the window. I stood there petrified. It took all my courage to run back to bed and pull the covers over my head. The next day, when I reported what I had seen, Pappa casually remarked: "There was no one there. You just imagined it." I refused to believe him, because in my mind what I saw was real. The idea that such an image could arise from my imagination and fear seemed impossible.

My sister Taimi and I were both placed into first grade. I do not recall learning German. Our family spoke Estonian at home, yet we children seemed to know how to speak German. As I think about it, I can see that, without consciously being aware of it, we had retained the ability to speak German from our nursery-school days at the monastery in Neresheim.

Hans was one grade above us. Boys and girls went to different schools. There were many children in our neighborhood to play with, and Sunday afternoons the Czerwenkas invited us to play with their grandchildren.

Mutti came home from the hospital with her leg in a cast. Grandmother tended to the household and Pappa had found a job in a textile factory, to which he rode his bicycle, four miles each way. We were just getting settled when our lives were interrupted again as the war moved closer.

IN THE PATH OF WAR

We had fled to Austria with the hope of escaping the communists. On arriving, however, we learned that the Red Army was approaching Austria from the north. We were in an active war zone and school was constantly interrupted by air raids. When the sirens began blaring our teacher would softly tell us to pick up our little blackboards, and then would lead us to the public shelter. In the shelter she would regale us with stories while we sat on long benches and waited for the all-clear signal. She was an older woman who, with her gentle voice and calmness, reassured us all that we had nothing to fear.

When we were at home and the sirens sounded we would dash into the cellar which had a dirt floor and two benches. Weeks went by when there was no school because of the constant air raids. On other days we would arrive in school and the piercing siren would alert us to seek shelter. We had no books, and I do not know how I learned to read, but by the end of first grade I could read well. We did have chalk and little individual blackboards on which we practiced our letters and did our math. When we were done we erased what we had written so we could start anew.

One day when we returned from school, Mutti was in the kitchen talking to a man I had never seen before. On the table were black, strangely shaped contraptions. It turned out they were gas masks. I counted them: there was one for each of us. When I placed mine over my face, I felt that I could not breathe. The rubber was tight around my nose and squeezed my mouth. My breath became rapid, and I was sure I was suffocating. I frantically pulled the mask off. Everyone needed to be prepared for the possibility of gas warfare. A rumor circulated in our part of Austria that either the Allies or the Germans would resort to using gas. We had gotten used to expecting bombs, but this was scarier. From now on we were to take our gas masks with us to the shelters. I was certain that, no matter what happened, I would refuse to put mine on. Fortunately we never had to use the gas masks.

After Adolph Hitler became chancellor of Germany in 1933 he ordered that people greet each other with "Heil Hitler." Even the letter from the German army doctor who had tended to my father as he was dying closed with "Heil Hitler" before the signature. My father concluded his letters with "Heil Hitler" since his letters were read by censors while he was in the army. To deviate from saying "Heil Hitler" would make one suspect of disloyalty to Hitler's cause.

Before the war the common Austrian greeting had been "Grüss Gott"—literally "God greet you," but ever since Nazi Germany annexed Austria in 1938 all Austrians were ordered to greet each other with the salutation "Heil Hitler" while raising their right arm. I could never remember which arm to lift up. Often I raised the left when it was always supposed to be the right.

One morning on our way to school, a tall, well-dressed man and a stylish woman were walking toward us. Both of us instinctively raised our arms and said, "Heil Hitler." I feared that if we did not say "Heil Hitler" we would get into trouble. What kind of trouble I didn't know, but I was not willing to take any chances. I faithfully kept saying "Heil Hitler" to everyone I passed. When the war ended on May 9, 1945, Austrians immediately returned to greeting each other with "Grüss Gott." We children understood that we were never to say "Heil Hitler" again.

Recently I asked Taimi what she remembered about the salutation. She adamantly stated that she had refused to say "Heil Hitler." I cannot believe that.

The war kept raging around us and we got used to the sirens going off. When we heard the familiar piercing sound we dropped everything and automatically ran for shelter. The bombing was coming closer. When the railroad hub three miles to the east in Attnang was severely bombed, our parents decided that it was no longer safe to stay in Vöcklabruck.

The Soviet Union had let it be known that all Estonians discovered living outside of Estonia would be immediately sent back. We knew, therefore, that if we were overrun by the Red Army, we would be forcibly repatriated.

RUNNING FROM THE RUSSIAN BEAR

Every evening our parents and grandmother were glued to the crackly little radio in the kitchen, hearing terrible stories about the total destruction of cities in Germany and Austria. I did not understand that the Americans, French, and British were allied with the Soviet Union and that all were trying to defeat the Germans. As a six year old I feared only the Red Army. The Soviets already had occupied Vienna and were moving steadily toward Upper Austria where we lived.

My parents agonized over what to do next. We had traveled far to get away from the Soviets and now they were rapidly coming toward us. Mutti and Pappa made the difficult decision to leave Vöcklabruck in order to stay ahead of the Red Army. Simultaneously, the Americans were approaching from the west, advancing from Salzburg toward Vöcklabruck, while the Red Army was pursuing the German army from the east, and there was no way to know who would get to Vöcklabruck first. We did not want to end up in the path of the Soviets. The Americans were our only hope.

After living seven months in Vöcklabruck we again packed our belongings and headed to the train station. We had no idea where we were going except that it would be west, ahead of the advancing Red Army. The train station was packed with people speaking different languages and, like us, fearing the Soviet advance. With this big mass of refugees, we managed, in April 1945, to board a train going west, toward the advancing Americans.

We left in the evening and by morning had traveled what turned out to be no more than 12 miles before the train stopped. Our train was filled with refugees all trying to get away. At first it seemed that this would be a short stop, but hours passed and we still were not moving. People were becoming anxious since everyone knew that time was of the essence. At last we were told officially why we could not travel on; the tracks ahead had been heavily bombed and were impassable. No one seemed to know how long repairs might take. The passengers were upset by the news, but all the more because next to our train was a long tanker train carrying oil. The overwhelming fear of all the passengers was that if the oil tankers were hit, everything around them would be destroyed. We were in an active war zone, with bombing all around us and the air-raid sirens constantly going off. As soon as we heard the sirens, we abandoned whatever we were doing and quickly ran in search of shelter. Frankenmarkt, the town where we were stopped, did not have enough shelters for all the train occupants, so it was vital to get to a shelter as quickly as possible. We had strict orders from our parents always to stay together and to not become separated.

One night the piercing sound of the sirens woke me up in the middle of a deep sleep. Grandmother grabbed my hand, Mutti took baby Annika, and Pappa was with Hans and Taimi. The confusion prevented us from staying together and none of us made it to a shelter. Grandmother and I ended up on a hillside with a large group of women and children. Whenever the planes came closer we all lay flat on the ground. Grandmother explained that if we lay flat there was less chance of the planes spotting us. We were all quiet, listening to the roar of airplanes overhead. Periodically I saw the sky light up and then I heard someone shout, "They are dropping Christmas trees." A lady nearby motioned to me to come to the edge of the hill to see them. I was too scared to look. Instead I closed my eyes as the sky brightened. We stayed on that hill for a long time. I learned later that what she called "Christmas trees" were aerial flares dropped by aircraft at night to illuminate targets to be bombed. Apparently they came in different colors and looked like falling candles. The standard description for them was indeed Christmas trees. Although I did not see them, referring to them as Christmas trees upset me. The only Christmas trees I knew were beautiful, lit with candles, and part of a happy holiday. This instead was a time when we were frightened and dashing for shelter to avoid the bombs. The roar of the airplanes was relentless and was followed by explosions to the west, the direction we were trying to go.

We were starting to run out of the provisions we had brought along. Although we had money, it was difficult to find anything to buy. After five days on the train we children overheard our parents talking about going back to Vöcklabruck. I liked the idea of returning to a life that was familiar and where I had friends. There was still no word as to when the tracks to Salzburg would reopen. We heard rumors that the Americans were advancing rapidly and might get to Vöcklabruck before the Russians. Mutti and Pappa decided that we would take the chance and try to return to Vöcklabruck. Pappa succeeded in contacting Mr. Czerwenka, who assured him that we could get our living quarters back.

We returned to Vöcklabruck—and stayed for seven years.

In my mind there clearly was still only one enemy: the Russians. I thought the Americans were coming solely to push the Russians back. What I did not understand, and what the world rightfully knew, was that the Nazis needed to be stopped and that the Allied bombing was initiated to defeat the German advance. Being a child, I could not grasp that living in Austria meant that *we were part of the enemy.*

The exodus of refugees kept coming through Vöcklabruck. They all had the same desire: to survive the war and to not end up under Soviet domination. A good number of the weary refugees who came through Vöcklabruck stayed. This was the reason we kept getting so many new students when I was in first and second grade. I heard that our family may well have

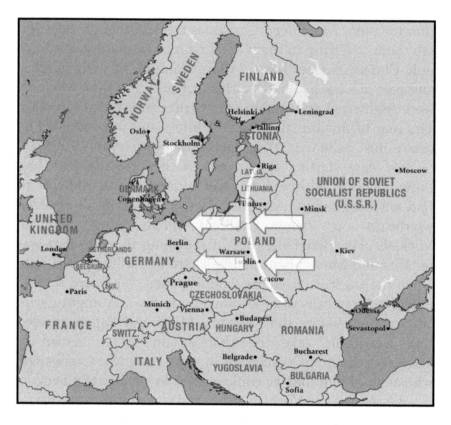

1944 and 1945 - The Soviet army pushed the German army back into Germany, occupying the Baltic States and most of Eastern Europe.

been the first refugee family to arrive in Vöcklabruck. Apparently the mayor did not want refugees and had urged Mr. Czerwenka to send us on our way. Fortunately, he refused.

At that time, no one had imagined that Vöcklabruck would become a center for refugees. There were the German evacuees from Hamburg and Dresden, whose houses had been destroyed in air raids. Then there were the Romanians, Hungarians, Bulgarians, and people of many other nationalities, along with the Austrians from Vienna, which the Red Army already had taken. We children would stand by the window and watch these people drudging along the road. Mostly they were women and children struggling to carry their belongings: the men were all fighting in the war or had lost their lives. We were excited one day when we saw a camel loaded down with suitcases. We had never seen a camel before and could not stop talking about it. There were covered wagons pulled by horses and people pushing carts, wheelbarrows, and baby carriages. Most people walked. Looking at their weary faces, it was evident that they had been walking for a long time.

I vividly recall the day the war ended, May 9, 1945. The radio was on in the morning, and people were advised to seek shelter. What was different was that no sirens were going off. We went into the cellar, but we must not have stayed there very long.

Instead, I remember a beautiful sunny day, and various scenes flash before my eyes. We are standing by the window looking at the emaciated, bedraggled German soldiers marching by. It is quiet outside. There are so many of them marching. Then there is a lull. Suddenly there is a loud roar, and people converge from all directions into the street and the park, laughing, screaming, crying, and dancing. I am puzzled by where they all are coming from and also run outside. I have not seen so many people in the street before.

People jubilantly yell, "The war is over!"

As I look to my right, next to the house, I see a man hand Pappa a cigarette. They light their cigarettes, smile, and talk while taking drags on their cigarettes. I have never seen Pappa smoke before. Then I see a convoy of jeeps driving down the street coming from the west. Each jeep holds muscular American soldiers grinning and waving. The crowd goes wild. We all wave and clap. These are our liberators. This is what we have been waiting for. As I look around, I see red-white-red striped flags flying everywhere. Where did they come from? Gone are the flags with swastikas. Instead, Austrian flags are fluttering from every house.

LIVING IN THE AMERICAN ZONE

When World War II ended, after five years of destruction and misery, there was great jubilation. The Nazi Third Reich was over. Hitler had committed suicide ten days earlier, when Berlin fell and he feared capture.

Austria, like Germany, was now divided into four military zones, as was the capital, Vienna. France, Britain, America, and Russia each assumed responsibility for its designated area. To our great joy, we were in the American zone. Yet my parents continued to be apprehensive, because the Red Army was poised only 40 miles northeast of Vöcklabruck.

Although the war was officially over, the political situation remained volatile. No one believed that the agreed-upon boundaries would hold. The USSR let it be known that all refugees from the three Baltic countries—Estonia, Latvia, and Lithuania—were to return to their homelands. My parents and grandmother were devastated when they heard about the Yalta agreements made in February of the same year, when Churchill, Roosevelt, and Stalin met to decide the political divisions of Europe after the war. The Atlantic Charter provisions that had given so much hope to Estonians were discarded and Estonia was to remain a part of the Soviet Union. The United States never officially acknowledged the Soviet Union's right to Estonia, yet the result of the Yalta agreement was that Estonia did not regain its independence and remained under Russian occupation.

All hope of returning to Estonia was now gone.

When my sister and I recently went through family papers, we came across an official document issued by the Military Government of Austria in July 1945, barely two months after the end of the war. It states: "Mr. Verner Toffer and family, claiming to be citizens of Estonia, and not citizens of Soviet Russia prior to 1939, are not required to go to Soviet Russia. Permission is given for the bearer to remain in Austria until a repatriation plan can be made for his or her nationality." This document was signed by an American displaced persons officer. It gave some assurance to my parents that they would have some legal protection in case their nationality came under question. Whether the Austrian government had the power to prevent our repatriation was never challenged.

Now that the Americans were in control of Upper Austria, their big concern was what to do with all the refugees who needed housing, work, and food. Vöcklabruck was named as one of the eight official refugee campsites in the small state of Upper Austria. Many of my new classmates lived in this camp, called Fluko-Lager.

Local people also had to make adjustments when the occupying Americans took over. Mr. Czerwenka was ordered to vacate his beautiful big villa, and it temporarily became an American command post. He and his family moved upstairs in the house where we were living. His son, Oskar, who must have been in his early 20s, also lived briefly above us. Oskar was an aspiring opera singer. We would often hear him singing early in the morning. Some days his deep bass voice would burst into magnificent arias from famous operas and Austrian operettas.

In time, Oskar became a well-known star with the Vienna State Opera. He also sang as a guest soloist with various other opera companies around the world, including the New York Metropolitan Opera. I was curious to see if I could hear his voice again and found Oskar on YouTube, where he is singing a touching Schubert song and an aria from Don Pasquale. *It was the same voice I had enjoyed as a young child.*

Pappa continued his job in a textile factory three miles away. He made the round trip daily on his bicycle. He had to carry an official paper stating that he had permission to ride his bicycle to and from work. In the following year, the American military government asked Pappa to re-establish in Vöcklabruck a textile mill that had burned several years before. The Americans had found out, most likely from Mr. Czerwenka, that Pappa was a textile engineer and had been part owner of a linen factory in Estonia. After the war, there was a great shortage of most items. Mr. Czerwenka later purchased the textile factory and turned the business over to Pappa. He named his son Oskar as director; since he was an aspiring opera singer and had no interest in the business, he was happy to have Pappa in charge. In time, Pappa created a successful business producing a variety of fabrics suited for mattress covers, bed linens, dresses and shirts, and some woolen fabrics for suits. He even added a wool-dyeing department to the factory.

The main square in Vöcklabruck

As I look back, I can see how fortunate our family was to have met Mr. Czerwenka's son-in-law, Mr. Mayerhofer, in Estonia. It was his letter of introduction to Mr. Czerwenka asking him to help us if we ever arrived on his doorstep in Vöcklabruck that made such a difference in our lives. I see now in how many ways Mr. Czerwenka's support, generosity, and respect for my parents helped us before and after the war.

Mr. Mayerhofer returned from military duty and soon thereafter moved with his family back to their home in Linz on the Danube River. Austria remained officially under Allied occupation until 1955, although the Austrian government gradually assumed most self-governing functions during the intervening ten years. Our family felt very lucky that the war ended before Vöcklabruck fell under Soviet domination. For our family, it meant that we could remain in Vöcklabruck, in the American zone.

LOOKING FOR FOOD

I don't remember being hungry. Yet most of my memories from the first year after the end of the war, when I turned seven, seem to involve food: finding food, gathering food, and overhearing talk of where food could be had. One time my nine-year-old brother located a stopped Hungarian supply train and came back with several pairs of lambskin mittens and disappointedly added that there was no food on the train. Another time Grandmother heard the rumor that people had broken into a warehouse where there might be food. She hurriedly grabbed a bag and dashed out. When she came home, the bag was filled with sugar. It was such a rare treat and I remember that on that day we were allowed to eat a whole spoonful. After this Grandmother rationed the sugar so that we could enjoy it longer.

For my seventh birthday I received a new doll. Somewhere between Danzig, Poland, and Vienna, I had sadly lost the doll I brought from Estonia. Many years later I heard that in order to get this doll for me, Mutti had bartered bed sheets and fabric that they had brought from Estonia. She had been able to make a trade with a woman whose daughter was a few years older than Taimi and me and who often played with us. My doll was made of celluloid, with short brown hair, a short-sleeved flowered dress and patent-leather shoes. I have kept her to this day.

Across from our house was a park. It was a great place for us children to play. For a while the American soldiers placed their field kitchen there. I could smell the bacon. Sometimes a few soldiers would sit on the curb outside our window. I would run outside and stand before them and watch them eat. Occasionally one of them would give me candy or a piece of chocolate, and one time I got a pancake. I heard that Mr. Czerwenka's daughter, Mrs. Mayerhofer, had admonished the soldiers for not sharing food with the starving children. I do not know if that is what prompted them, but the soldiers began to hand out leftover food from their big cooking pots and pans. There were always lots of skinny kids around patiently waiting. We were thrilled with whatever was given to us. After the soldiers moved out of the park, the people living around the park turned it into a vegetable garden.

One day I overheard some older kids say that an outdoor food kitchen was being set up a few blocks away. I ran inside, grabbed a cup and spoon, and headed to the food kitchen, only to discover that throngs of people were already there. I pushed my way forward. Finally I managed to get closer and was able to reach my cup toward a man who was giving out string beans. Several landed in my cup. As I pulled my hand back, I scratched my palm on the edge of the big pan. Pain shot through me. There was no more food to be had and the kitchen closed. When I got home, Mutti tended to my wound.

Two days later, I noticed that there was a red line creeping up my forearm. I looked at it with fascination as it crept further. I finally mentioned it to Mutti, who calmly said that I had blood poisoning and had to see a doctor. My brother, who had an infected thumb from having hit it with a hammer, and I would walk together to the clinic at the hospital. We each made a number of visits before our infections were under control.

We all became adept at finding anything edible in the nearby fields and woods. Somehow we learned where raspberry and blueberry bushes were, where to search for mushrooms, where to find apples, and to scour the fields for something we could eat. Grandmother was able to transform weeds and grasses we had foraged into soup. My siblings and I would invariably argue about who had the most bubbles of fat in their soup. Rarely did any of us spot more than three or four tiny specs because there was no fat to put into the soup.

I made a big find one afternoon not too far from our home. Where the sidewalk met the street, I saw half a loaf of bread. It looked like someone had taken a few bites and then thrown the rest away. I picked up the dirty loaf and took it home. Mutti and Grandmother were so excited. They removed the crust and eaten part, sliced the bread, and warmed it in the oven. I felt so proud when we all shared my special find. I was sure that this was the very best bread I had ever had.

It is only in looking back that I understand why I do not remember being hungry. No doubt there were many times when we were hungry, like everyone else trying to survive. Yet we children must have understood that our parents and grandmother were doing everything in their power to provide for us. We trusted that things would get better.

Gradually things did get better. In school we began to receive hot soup and occasionally hot chocolate, most likely distributed by UNICEF. We also received occasional packages from the Red Cross and CARE. My favorites were the CARE packages. These packages were a highlight for us children because they contained chocolate and crackers, and pencils and toothbrushes, and other necessities. One time I received what I later learned was a game of jacks. I had no idea what to do with the eight jacks and the little red ball, and instead I made up my own games.

When these special packages arrived, it was quite common for friends to stop by to celebrate the occasion. One time I overheard the grown-ups talking about a man who had received a big tin of saltine crackers. He had been so ravenous that he ate them all, drinking a lot of water while doing so.

This had been too much for his empty stomach, which had exploded. For all of us living on starvation diets, this was a scary reminder that eating too much too quickly could have dire consequences.

Austria had endured much damage during the war, with many factories, towns, roads, and railroad tracks destroyed. Fortunately, around where we lived, there was not much visible damage. Vöcklabruck, however, like so many other towns in Austria, was dealing with a big influx of refugees. The war also took its toll on the physical and emotional well-being of the locals and refugees. I have heard it said that every family had lost someone who was dear to them during the war. Yet for most people, during the first year or two after the war, getting enough to eat was the predominant concern.

Later I learned that right after the war the official food rations were at first 1,100 calories daily for each person and then were reduced to 800 calories. The rations consisted mostly of lentils and dried peas. In addition, each person was allotted one slice of bread per day, and every family had a meat ration for one meal a week.

Since the Czerwenkas were living upstairs with his sister and her husband, it became clear that we needed to find other housing. We all lived there during the summer until a small, unheated house was found for us behind the milk store in what was considered the outskirts of town. The Czerwenkas were then able to use the rooms we had vacated until they got their home back from the American military.

This was to be a temporary move for us. I recall that we were all very cold and cramped that winter. I liked living in this part of town, though, because several of my classmates lived nearby. We had much freedom to explore the countryside, play in the nearby woods, and enjoy great sledding on the big hill nearby.

WITNESS TO CRUELTY

Certain memories remain vivid forever. I can think of two—when I was seven years old—that had a great impact on me. As I look back, I realize that these two memories were pivotal in determining the direction I chose for my life.

I was in second grade in the Vöcklabruck elementary school. My teacher was Herr Huber, who was also the school principal. We girls went to school in the morning. The war had ended the spring before. The picture of Adolf Hitler in front of the classroom, which was next to the crucifix, had been replaced by a beautiful picture of the Virgin Mary. I went to a public school in Austria, where Catholicism was the official religion of the country. This was the time of grave food shortages and around 10:30 every morning came a knock on the classroom door. A big round steel pot, usually filled with some kind of hot soup and occasionally hot chocolate, was brought into our room. We children lined up in single file and presented our cups, which we had brought from home. Mine was speckled blue enamel.

Herr Huber scared me. He was a very serious man, talked in a loud voice, and expected order and silence. We all stood up when he walked into the room, and stood until he reached the front of the classroom. He wore suits and smelled of cigarette smoke. Occasionally he would call on us children to recite something. I feared that he might call on me. When he did, I was expected to stand up and answer the question. My answers were inaudible whispers. He would bellow at me, "Louder! Louder!" We still had no books and continued to use our little handheld blackboards to do math problems and write sentences. During the latter part of the school year we received limited access to pencils, paper, and even inkwells, into which we dipped our newly acquired pens.

My seat was near a window toward the back of the room. In front of me sat Greta, who had joined our class several months before. One day as we were copying something on our blackboards, Herr Huber suddenly stopped talking. He began to walk toward Greta and me. I was scared and wondered if I had done something. He stopped at Greta's desk and said angrily, "How many times have I told you that you have to write with your right hand? You know it is forbidden to write with your left hand." Greta was now standing, as we had been instructed to do, and held her head down clutching her hands. He continued: "Hold out your left hand." Then I noticed he had a steel ruler in his hand. He slapped it down hard on her hand several times. Greta said nothing. He continued: "I don't ever want to see you write with your left hand again." Greta did not answer. He glared at her and struck her hand again and again. Greta began to cry.

I do not remember how many times he struck her, but for a long time afterwards I could see and hear the ruler smack down on Greta's hand. I was one of the children who had had a hard time deciding if I was right- or left-handed. By second grade I was clearly right-handed. I will never know if I became right-handed because I had already absorbed the belief, common at that time, that to be left-handed was going against God's will and letting the devil win. There seemed to be something disturbing about being left-handed.

The newcomers to our class all seemed to be living in a camp set up by the American military to house refugees. A former air-space monitoring center, no longer needed for that purpose after the war, became what was known as the Fluko-Lager. The camp apparently had its own school for the younger children. Since the school was not accredited, students in the latter part of the school year came to the public school so that they could be promoted to the next grade. Maria was one of these children. We all were in awe of the beautiful black hair that she wore woven into one long pigtail that she could almost sit on. She had recently joined my second grade class and we ran into each other one day on the town square. We each had with us our younger sisters. Her sister had the same dark hair but she wore it cut short just past her ears. The four of us walked around together looking at shop windows while talking and laughing.

One morning, Herr Huber was late coming to class. That had never happened before. He walked slowly to the front of the class. He said to us that one of our classmates would no longer be coming to school. He then told us that she had been killed the night before. It was Maria, the girl with whom I had been in the town square. A girl who lived in the same camp piped up, "She and her sister were both killed. It was their stepfather who did it. He chased them outside and they couldn't get away." Herr Huber did not reprimand her for just blurting out the news. Instead, that was the only day I remember him being kind and soft-spoken. Several days later our whole class went to the funeral held at the Schöndorfer Kirche, the big Catholic Church up on the hill. We walked there as a class, with Herr Huber leading the way. Many people came to the church. We stood outside the church door as the two little caskets were carried in. In a procession, we walked in and sat together during the Catholic mass for the dead.

I was upset and confused by the death of my classmate. It wasn't that she had been sick or had been in an accident. That I could have understood. Instead, she was killed by her step-father, a person who was supposed to take care of her. When we talked about it at home, my parents said that sometimes people did terrible things because of their own demons. I did not understand what that meant. Up to that point I only knew that terrible things happened during the war. I had learned that the Russians killed people and did awful things. I did not yet know of all the other atrocities committed in that same war. Although I did not understand, it seemed that the killings during the war were for a greater purpose, but murdering a child just because one is troubled seemed incomprehensible. What made such an evil act possible? Could this act not have been prevented? I was also bothered by the fury that Herr Huber showed toward Greta. How could he be so cruel to her? Did he think he was saving her from Satan?

I continued to try to understand what made people do what they did. For this curiosity I was at times reprimanded for being nosy. I concluded that there was something shameful about my interest. More than a dozen years later, while in college, I became aware that there were careers in which one could help people find better ways to deal with their demons rather than expressing them through cruelty. The path I eventually chose was that of a clinical social worker specializing in psychotherapy.

THE POCKET KNIFE

In the spring of 1946 we moved into our own house across the street from the little house where we had spent the very cold winter. This house had a fence all the way around it. In the front yard was a vegetable garden, and in the back and on the sides were plum and apple trees and gooseberry and currant bushes.

One day my sister found a pocketknife. She had gone to the store and on the way back she found this little knife on the street. She showed it to me. Its color was soft beige and it had one large blade and one small blade. I was jealous. I wanted my own pocketknife. I proclaimed, "I am going out and I will find one too!" Then I added: "I will go look up around the church." Both my sisters followed.

Annika, me, and Taimi

Our house was located at what at that time was considered the edge of town. Behind the house a path led through a meadow up to a high hill. On the top of the hill was a magnificent old church, the Schöndorfer Kirche, surrounded by a cemetery. This Roman Catholic Church was built in the year 824 and was considered the principal landmark of the town. What intrigued us children were the wrought iron enclosures protruding several feet from the sides of the church. They contained bones that had been taken out of their graves to make room for new remains. What always gave us the shivers was to walk past the one that held the skulls, which were carefully piled up, with initials and a date written on top of each skull. These skulls faced us, and the empty sockets looked as if they were staring right at us. There were hundreds of them! The bones that belonged to the skulls were equally carefully marked and arranged in other enclosures.

The church was not where I headed this time. I ran over to the potato fields nearby. There were long furrows of potato plants. In the spring my class had come up there to collect potato beetles, which we placed into glass jars. It was the job of all the local school children to collect the beetles so that they would not destroy the crop. By now the potatoes had already been harvested.

Schöndorfer Kirche in Vöcklabruck

We saw an old man with straggly hair and a long beard, wearing dirty pants, suspenders, and a torn coat, walking through the furrows, pushing plants aside as if he were looking for something. Occasionally he would pick something up and put it into his pocket, most likely a potato. We ran around the furrows chasing each other. He looked at us as if he wanted to say something. We made sure not to get too close to him. He kept walking up and down the furrows with his eyes cast down. Suddenly my eyes spotted something shiny. I leaned down and I could not believe it—there was a pocketknife. It was dirty black, with a silver edge that reflected the rays of the sun. I jumped up and down yelling to my sisters, "I found it, I found it." Immediately we ran down the hill and headed home.

Years later I thought of that incident in the potato fields. I do not recall what prompted it. I suddenly realized that the old man must have been looking for his knife. The day we were up at the potato fields was shortly after the war. This may well have been the only knife he had. When I opened up the blades, I saw how worn they were.

Did he actually call out to us when I had screamed in jubilation? I do not remember. I just took off with my coveted find. Apart from the initial joy at also finding a pocketknife, the knife meant nothing to me and soon was lost. For me, finding a pocketknife was simply a competitive challenge with my sister. My joy at the sheer luck of finding a pocketknife overtook any consideration that what I found might have been exactly what the old man was searching for.

THE DAY I STOPPED CRYING

How is it possible that I remember the day I stopped crying and have no recollection of why I was crying? I was in the kitchen in our house in Austria. Grandmother was by the stove adding more coal. The ironing board was up while the iron warmed on the stove. My younger sister, Annika, sat at the table coloring. I sobbed loudly, with my chest heaving every time I caught my breath. It did not seem to matter if it was a small slight or something that deeply upset me, my cry was the same: loud and long.

Grandmother looked at me and said sternly, "Stop your howling." I was taken aback. She rarely, if ever, raised her voice to me. I kept crying. Grandmother raised the iron, and repeated, "I said, stop your howling!" I continued to cry. "Do you want your father to turn himself over in his grave?" were her next words. I stopped abruptly. I felt a shiver go through my body. Grandmother continued with her ironing.

Inwardly I was confused as strange images flashed through my mind. My father—her son—had been killed in action in World War II, three years earlier, when I was five years old. In my mind I tried to visualize him dressed in a soldier's uniform as I remember him, in a coffin. Or would he be all bandaged up because he had been injured? The next moment, I saw a skull and bones rattling in a coffin just like the ones we had seen many times around the Schöndorfer Kirche. I said nothing of what I was experiencing. Grandmother kept ironing, Annika continued coloring. I tried to imagine how my father could turn himself around in his coffin just because I was sobbing. Could he really hear me? Was he up in heaven, aware of what I was doing? These were all new ideas. My thoughts were interrupted when my sister Taimi ran in the door: "Aren't you two coming out?" Annika and I jumped up and ran outside.

Looking back, I can see that this interchange with my grandmother, whom I loved, dried up my tears almost for good. It became hard for me to cry at funerals, although I would feel profound sadness and grief. At other times, when something touching happens, especially in movies, my tears flow easily. I wonder now what was going on with Grandmother that prompted her to respond to my sobbing with such impatience. Had she been thinking of my father? Could it have been around his birthday or some other anniversary? What made her utter such a threat? I do not believe that it ever occurred to her that I would take her threat literally and stop crying because otherwise *my father might turn himself over in his grave.*

I COMMIT A SIN

When do we develop the concept of sin? I have been looking back at my life trying to recall when I first felt that I had committed a sin. As I consider this, I remember one specific occasion when I felt the earliest flush of recognition that I had done something so shameful that it had to be a sin.

I was eight years old. We were living in our new house in Vöcklabruck. The war had ended about a year and a half earlier. Food was still in short supply. Compared to what it had been like the previous two years, life was easier.

I was going for a walk with Grandmother, Vera, her new friend, and Annika, my four-year-old sister. Vera was an Estonian woman who appeared at our house and stayed around for a while. Full-figured, tall, with billowing blond hair, she loved to talk and was full of entertaining stories. Vera had a commanding presence. She was the first person on whose every word I hung. That day she had on a striped skirt and a low-cut blouse. We walked past the houses into the countryside. On our right was a road that curved up a hill to a farmhouse. Vera wistfully said, "I wonder if they have any eggs?" She turned to me: "I know you would like some eggs. Why don't you take Annika and go up to the farm and ask for eggs." I looked at Grandmother and she nodded, saying, "Just ask for two." I hesitated. Grandmother said to Annika, "You go with her." I didn't want to go, yet felt impelled to do as I was told.

I took Annika's hand and we walked slowly up the hill to the farmhouse. I knocked timidly on the door. A large woman appeared and let us in. My voice was shaking, but I managed to ask her for two eggs. "Do you have money?" I shook my head. She glared at me, with her voice rising, "Who sent you up here to beg?" My face felt flushed and I whispered, "No one sent me—it was my idea." I wanted to bolt out the door. She shook her head, adding, "I don't believe you." I held Annika's hand tighter and turned to leave. "Wait a minute," she said. I stopped abruptly and watched her leave the room. When she returned, she handed me two white eggs.

I hesitated to take them. I felt ashamed: I knew I had lied and begged. I held the two fragile eggs in one hand, grasping Annika's hand even harder, and we ran down the hill. I handed the eggs to Vera, who smiled broadly and told me that I did well. I don't recall Grandmother saying anything.

At that time, I felt that I had committed a sin. I had been learning about the Ten Commandments in school. Although I went to a public school, there was a crucifix on the wall of our classroom, and we began the school day with the Lord's Prayer. Once a week a priest came to teach religion. My Lutheran classmates and I went to another room where we were taught by the pastor from our church.

I knew that one commandment decrees, "Thou shall not steal." I felt that I had done something that might be even worse: I had begged. When there had been such a shortage of food right after the war, I had never resorted to begging. Instead I had felt good about being resourceful in doing my share to help find food and contribute to the family.

As I look back at this incident, I am puzzled by my grandmother's behavior. She had agreed that I go up to the farmhouse and ask for eggs. Without Vera's presence, I am certain she would not have suggested that I go there. Had she also fallen under the spell of Vera and been unable to resist her?

What was it about Vera that made her so persuasive? I wonder now: what did she go through in order to survive during the war? What had she been like before? Had she learned to use her body and had she developed a cunning mind in order to have enough to eat and make it through the war alive? There was something about Vera that made her hard to refuse. She was attractive, charming, and no doubt flirtatious. As a child I admired her. What mattered to her was that I had succeeded and brought back eggs. The fact that I had to beg to get them and was uncomfortable probably did not cross her mind. Although it made me feel like a sinner, in her eyes I was a good girl.

A PACKAGE FROM AMERICA

When the war ended, the Allies who now occupied Germany had to decide what to do with all the refugees. Their solution was to gather together people by nationalities and house them in small towns until they could be resettled. The village of Geislingen in southern Germany was designated as the displaced persons (DP) camp for Estonians. German residents in three sections of the town were ordered to evacuate their homes for the arriving Estonians. Single houses became homes for multiple families who shared the kitchen and bathrooms. I am impressed by what I have read about this Geislingen community of Estonians. They quickly opened schools for the children, formed an orchestra and theater and folk-dancing groups, started a newspaper, and did so much to normalize life. I don't know the details of my godfather Arnold's journey, but he too ended up in Geislingen, where he put his newspaper skills to good use.

The hope of every Estonian in Geislingen was to be resettled in one of the countries that was accepting refugees—Australia, New Zealand, the United States, Canada, Argentina, and Brazil. All the countries that opened their doors to immigrants were very far away from Estonia.

In order to gain entrance to the United States, one had to have a sponsor who promised employment and a place to live. Uncle Arnold, a newspaperman and writer, accepted a job offer from a fishing-boat captain in Miami, Florida. The first time we heard from Uncle Arnold we received a postcard with a picture of a palm tree and a colorful parrot. We children were in awe of this exotic place that he had moved to.

One day when Taimi and I returned from school, Mutti excitedly told me that I had received a package from America.

On the table was a big box wrapped in paper and addressed to me. The sender was my godfather, Uncle Arnold, from Miami, Florida. I remember trembling as I began to tear at the paper. My siblings and Mutti and Grandmother watched me eagerly. Annika said, "Open it! Open it!" What could possibly be in such a big box?

When I opened it up, I had no idea what to make of the contents. I had expected candies or cookies or something to eat or wear, but that's not what I found. There were two bulbous-shaped, greenish-brown things about ten inches in diameter. I was totally mystified. Then Mutti called out, "They are coconuts!" I had never in my life seen a coconut. These two coconuts were still surrounded by the outer husk. Mutti turned to me and said, "Try shaking one." I did. I could hear liquid moving inside the coconut. Taimi and Hans passed the other one around, shaking it and marveling at the size of the coconut. My initial disappointment disappeared when I realized I had received a gift that had actually grown on a palm tree in Florida. When Pappa came home from work, he also was impressed by the coconuts. My parents knew about coconuts, of course, but they had never seen one still in the husk. That evening we all took turns trying to open up one of the coconuts. It was hard work to remove the husk. Finally we reached the inner nut. I marveled at the hard brown shell and decided not to crack it open so that I could take it to school and show it to my classmates.

When I showed them the coconut in the husk and the other one with the husk removed, they were all impressed. Everyone, including children and teachers in the other classes, wanted to touch them. No one had ever seen an unopened coconut. I was usually shy, but I distinctly recall enjoying being the center of so much attention. That evening we all gathered in the kitchen and Hans gave the coconut a whack. The liquid began to ooze out. I quickly got a bowl and caught most of the milk. With the coconut now open, Mutti cut pieces for us all. It was hard to bite, but we ate every bit of it. It was an unfamiliar taste, but I thought it was delicious.

Mutti suggested that I donate the other coconut to the little museum at our elementary school. The museum consisted of one small room that we sometimes visited as part of our science lessons. There were drawers full of mounted colorful butterflies, different varieties of rocks, and a big collection of stuffed birds of various sizes. To this collection I added my prized coconut.

OUR OWN HOME

Only when we moved into our own home did I grasp that the war was really over. I associate moving into our new house with Austria becoming our new homeland. We were no longer cramped into one bedroom where I had to sleep against the wall next to Grandmother. There was more food in the stores. Pappa had a job rebuilding a textile factory that was going to begin producing much-needed fabrics. And best of all, we had our own home with a garden and apple and plum trees.

I saw how beautiful the area around us was when we took trips to nearby lakes and mountains. Our excursions were no

Our own home

longer geared to searching for mushrooms and berries so we would have something to eat. Now, when we looked for them, it was because we loved to eat them. We lived close to the picturesque mountainous countryside that is so well captured in the movie *The Sound of Music*.

Around the house was a fence. We came in through a wooden gate and entered from a door on the side. In the entryway was a sink with running cold water. This was the only water available to us. Straight ahead was my parent's bedroom. To the left was a kitchen and behind it another bedroom. From the entryway, stairs led up seven steps to the toilet on the left, and if you turned right, there were stairs that took you to the second floor, which was a big attic. In that big space, soon after we moved in, a room was built for Taimi and me. Having my own bed and a room for just the two of us seemed like such a luxury.

We also had a cellar with thick walls and a dirt floor. This is where food was kept cold, since we did not have a refrigerator. In the fall a farmer brought over a big supply of apples and potatoes that were stored on shelves in the cellar. The cellar never got so cold that the apples and potatoes froze. Grandmother and Mutti harvested the cabbage from our garden, cut it up, and submerged it in a brine solution in a big wooden barrel so it could ferment into sauerkraut. There was also a metal barrel filled with fresh eggs preserved in a water-glass solution. Mutti had explained to me that this was a method commonly used in Estonia to preserve eggs. Water-glass is the common name for sodium silicate. Eggs placed into the diluted water-glass solution stay fresh because no oxygen can enter through the pores of the shells. One year Grandmother and Mutti salted big pieces of pork and stacked them into a barrel for us to eat throughout the winter.

Our kitchen had a stove, heated with wood and coal, and a typical Austrian bench that curved around the back and on two sides, surrounding a large table. This was the room where we spent the most time: eating, doing homework, playing board games, cooking, ironing, and boiling laundry.

The house was built of stone and the walls must have been ten inches thick. The kitchen window usually had some plants in it. I loved sitting on the open windowsill in the bedroom next door. From there I had a perfect view of the Traunstein, a mountain about 15 miles away and nearly 6,000 feet high. To be living in this mountainous region was so different from our homeland, Estonia, where the highest mountain was not quite 1,000 feet high. What fascinated me was that most days the Traunstein seemed so close, and then on foggy overcast days it might disappear altogether.

Each of the two bedrooms had a big tile oven that had to be stoked regularly with coal to keep us warm in the winter. Our bedroom upstairs had a smaller stove, while the rest of the attic was unheated.

One time I took it upon myself to clear out the ashes from our bedroom stove. I thought I was being helpful. When Grandmother came upstairs and saw what I was doing, she became upset with me. Her fear was that I would start a fire, since there were a few embers among the ashes. The idea that I could potentially have started a fire traumatized me. I never emptied ashes again.

Taimi and I had one chore that we both dreaded. We had a vegetable garden in the front yard. In the spring, when it was planting time, Pappa insisted that we pick up the manure dropped by the horses pulling wagons down our street. He stressed that this was the best manure for growing cucumbers. We would both run out into the street with our little shovels and a stick looking around to make sure that none of our friends would be walking by. We did not gather much horse manure, but the vegetables grew well, and it may have had to do just as much with the fact that the garden had a lot of earthworms and snails. For a while, one of my amusements was to pick up a few snails, line them up in a row in a flat area, and watch the snails race each other to the finish line I had created. In addition to cucumbers, we raised tomatoes, potatoes, kohlrabi, cabbage, carrots, some herbs, and always flowers.

The back yard had plum trees, apple trees, gooseberry and raspberry bushes, and a small plot of grass where the laundry-drying lines were strung. My favorite tree was a tall apple tree right outside our front door. I loved to climb practically to the top of the tree, carrying a book to read. From there I could also see the street and whoever was passing by and feel assured that no one knew I was up there.

Our house had no bathtub or shower. Every Saturday Mutti would take us to the public baths, which belonged to the Eternit factory just a few blocks from our house. There we were given a towel and usually had to wait until a room became available. The mother of one of my classmates had the job of washing out the tubs and getting them ready for the next group. The men and boys entered their bath area through a separate door. Mutti would often say that we were fortunate that we had access to the public baths.

Although the war was officially over, our parents were still anxious about our future, since the Russians were only 40 miles away. Periodically there were threats and agitation, and peace seemed tenuous.

Austria was still divided into four zones: the French, British, Russian, and American, and no one knew how long the occupation would last. Since Estonia was now part of the Soviet Union, there was no way we could return to our homeland. We exiles in Austria received official cards certifying that we fell under United Nations jurisdiction. Most refugees in Austria, including our family, began to explore how to obtain legal entry to countries that were opening their doors to immigrants.

RED SUEDE SHOES

War rips families apart. Once separated, it is hard to find out what has become of relatives and friends. Not knowing creates an aching void. Grandmother and Mutti worried about what had happened to my Aunt Liidi and her family. Aunt Liidi was Mutti's sister. When we left Estonia in 1944, we had heard that Aunt Liidi, her husband, and their young son had escaped from Estonia in a small boat to Finland, a risky journey of 53 miles. In Estonia Aunt Liidi had been a physician and her husband a newspaper columnist and writer. Mutti discovered that the Red Cross organization had a program that traced missing family members. Like so many other people searching for their loved ones, Mutti met with a Red Cross worker and gave her the limited information she had. To our great joy, months later, a letter postmarked from Finland arrived from Aunt Liidi. The Red Cross had indeed succeeded in reconnecting our families. Shortly after that initial contact, Aunt Liidi and her family, now with two little boys, moved to Sweden. Russia was putting pressure on Finland to repatriate Estonians. Instead of cooperating with the Russians the Finns warned the Estonians, who were then taken in by Sweden. Life must have been easier in Sweden, because Aunt Liidi started to send us packages, always making sure to include a couple of bags of candy—a real luxury for us.

In the spring of 1948, when I was nine years old, Aunt Liidi and her family wanted to visit us in Vöcklabruck. There were obstacles to obtaining the proper visas and they were unable to get an entry visa to Austria. Then Mr. Czerwenka, who had so graciously helped our family when we arrived as refugees, found a way to get them over the border. He organized an illegal crossing from Germany, through a farmer's stable, and over a brook into Austria. Once across the border, he had a car waiting to drive them to our house. My cousins, eight- and six-year-old boys, loved their real-life adventure. After their visit with us, they again had to negotiate the same illegal crossing back into Germany. There was great joy and relief when we heard that Aunt Liidi and her family had escaped the border patrols and were safely back in Sweden.

Aunt Liidi and Mutti in the mountains near Vöcklabruck

Aunt Liidi, of course, brought us all presents. I received a pair of red suede shoes. They were a kind of sandal with a closed toe and a strap around my ankle. When I put them on, I felt like a princess. This is how Cinderella must have felt when she first put on her glass slipper. They were the most beautiful shoes I had ever seen. I had a pair of very ordinary brown shoes, hand-me-downs that did not fit well. Most of the time, when the weather was warm, we walked around barefoot, even to school. Now I could not stop looking at my feet. I proudly wore my new shoes to school where my classmates admired them. Much to my joy I was able to continue wearing my red suede shoes for a long time, because the expandable straps accommodated my growing feet.

SCHOOL DAYS

Our elementary school had become overcrowded when I started fourth grade, so room was found for us on the ground floor of a convent about three-quarters of a mile from the school. We heard that at one time our classroom had been part of the convent stables. The walls were thick and the small windows were high up, with metal bars over them. It was hard to imagine that there had been horses there. Occasionally we saw nuns walking by outside. The convent had an inner court and a church on the north end, where we never went. My classmates and I thought it was very special to have our own school.

I struggled with long division, but enjoyed learning almost everything else. This was also the year when, as I look back, I became more aware of myself. I was more self-conscious and sensitive and worried about who liked me and who didn't.

At home, in the evenings before we went to sleep, Mutti would often read us a chapter or two from books she had borrowed from the library. She loved Charles Dickens, and she read to us *A Christmas Carol*, *David Copperfield*, and *Oliver Twist*, all in German. The book that had the greatest impact on me was *Oliver Twist*. Oliver was an orphan. I began to wonder if I was also an orphan. I knew that my mother had died just before I turned two and my father when I was five. Yet technically, as far as I knew, I had already been adopted before he died. So in reality I was never an orphan, yet I had lost both my parents. I never asked about my parents. I really did want to ask, but somehow had concluded that, if I did, Mutti and Pappa might think I was ungrateful. After all, Mutti, who was my father's sister, and her family had adopted me and definitely treated me like one of their children.

My sister Taimi and I were in the same class through third grade, but then she skipped fourth grade. She went on to the Hauptschule—main school in German—which included fifth through eighth grades. Not having Taimi in my class meant that I had to rely more on myself. I had good friends in school. In addition, being in the only class that had been transferred to the former horse stable made us feel special.

Several memories from that school year remain vivid for me. One morning our teacher told us that our classmate Trudi would not be coming back to school for a while because of a family crisis. We all wondered what had happened. Monika, who lived near Trudi, blurted out, "Trudi's mother took an axe and attacked Trudi's Dad while he was sleeping. An ambulance came and took him to the hospital. Trudi and her mother ran away." I was appalled and fascinated by what I was hearing. I kept wondering what had prompted this woman to take such drastic measures. Trudi never returned to our class.

Every day my friend Frieda would meet me at my house, and we would walk to school. Sometime during the school year we began to stop at a bakery after school. We did that at least once or twice a week. We always asked for yeast. The baker would cut us a little slice from a big cake of yeast. He charged us very little, and we would both eagerly eat the yeast on our way home. I am sure we did that for many months. Thinking back on that time, what I remember is that we craved yeast. I wonder now if we both lacked vitamin B and instinctively realized that yeast, which is rich in vitamin B, provided what our bodies needed. The bakery had a wonderful aroma of fresh bread and rolls. We did not look at them, however, and always asked for the yeast.

A road separated our classroom from the river Vöckla. On sunny days we would eat our snack up on the embankment and look at the river below. Our teacher taught us all our subjects except religion. I do not remember any religious instruction in the fourth grade, yet it is hard for me to believe that we didn't have it. We still did not have textbooks, so we copied everything our teacher taught us into notebooks. When fourth grade ended, we moved on to the Hauptschule, which was a whole new school experience.

THE DAY I SURPRISED MYSELF

I n fifth grade we girls went to school on Tuesday, Thursday, and Saturday from 7:30 a.m. to 5 p.m. The boys attended the same school on Monday, Wednesday, and Friday. Latin was an elective class that was offered on Mondays. We met in a small room in the basement of the school. I did not really care for Latin, but it was better than being home on Monday, which was laundry day at our house. Grandmother and Mutti would heat a big kettle on the coal stove where they boiled sheets and all our clothes. We did not have a washing machine, nor did we have hot water. It was strenuous work and invariably they would become irritated with each other and us children if we got in their way or made any demands. Before the laundry could be hung outside to dry, Grandmother and Mutti had to wring out the water. In the winter the sheets hanging on the lines would become stiff in the freezing air.

I well remember a specific Latin class that had nothing to do with learning Latin. I had brought in my prize possession, a gold ballpoint pen that could write in red, blue, or black ink simply by pushing down separate little levers. I had found this beautiful pen. One day during the summer, I was in the post office, and as I went up to the teller, I noticed a golden pen on the floor. I picked it up and admired it—I had not seen a ballpoint pen before, although I had heard about them. We used pens that we dipped into little inkpots. And I had no idea that a pen could write in different colors. I told the teller I had found this pen and she simply said someone must have dropped it. There were no customers near us, so she said it was up to me what I did with it.

I wanted it so badly, but thought it must be valuable. I knew that there was a police station close by. I had previously noticed that, on the wall outside the station, there was an information case with a glass front. Inside it were posted various news articles and a typed sheet listing recently found items of sundry values. I went to the police station and showed the officer my find. He carefully examined the pen and said he would add it to the items listed, and if no one claimed it in 90 days, it would be mine. For a while I apprehensively checked daily to see if the pen had been claimed. As time went by, I dared to hope that one day this pen would be mine. On the ninety-first day, I became the owner of this beautiful, golden ballpoint pen. That evening I crocheted a little bag for it.

I took my golden pen to Latin class, where my classmates greatly admired it. Before class, several girls tried writing with it, making sure to try every color. One girl in particular loved my pen and didn't want to stop writing. We had a two-hour class with a brief outdoor break in the middle. When we came back in, I couldn't find my pen. I was pretty sure I had left it inside, but began to doubt my memory.

I stood up and said to our teacher, Mr. Weiss, "My pen is gone!" Mr. Weiss had us all look around, to no avail. I then said, "I want to go outside and look for my pen." He did not want to excuse me. I stood up, looked directly at him, and said, "I will not go home until I have found my pen." He knew me to be a student who was shy, who never volunteered or asked questions. There must have been something about the way I said it that made him believe me. I began to walk out. He told the whole class to follow me. We walked around where we had been and looked between the nearby bushes and in the grass. Suddenly there was a cry, "I found it!" And here was one of my classmates holding up my pen. It was the girl who had so admired my pen earlier in the day. I had my suspicion that this girl might have taken my pen, but I did not think I had the right to accuse her. I was glad that I had insisted that I would not leave until I had my pen back and also that I did not have to accuse the girl I suspected of taking it. Since she "found" it and handed the pen back to me, I was happy to have my prized possession again.

At home there were renewed concerns about the political situation in Europe. One evening as we were having dinner, Mutti said:

"The Russians are at it again."

"What did they do now?" Grandmother asked.

"They have blocked off all rail and road traffic to Berlin."

"That is just like them: they will do whatever they want," Pappa added.

I could see that they were visibly anxious about the news. As of June 24, 1948, the only access to Berlin, deep inside the Soviet zone, was by air. In order to get food and needed materials to the American, British, and French zones in Berlin, America and other Western countries had started a massive airlift program. It puzzled me that Mutti and Pappa were upset since I knew that Berlin was quite far from us.

"What if they blockade Vienna next?"

I had forgotten that Vienna, like Berlin, was also divided into four zones. Our parents were concerned that the blockade in Berlin could signal renewed Soviet expansion.

"What if they cross the border at Linz?" asked Hans.

Now this was close. The Russian zone was only 40 miles from us. We were in a direct path if the Soviets decided to ignore the boundaries established after the war. My parents and grandmother, based on their experience, were convinced that Russian leaders could not be trusted. I again felt vulnerable and that the Russian Bear was after us, something I had not thought of for quite a while.

The Soviet Union lifted the Berlin blockade after a fifteen-month standoff. Europe entered a period that became known as the Cold War.

VISITORS FROM FINLAND

I woke up early. It was still dark outside and the house was very quiet. This was the day when they were coming. Three weeks before, a letter had arrived in a blue envelope postmarked from Finland. Mr. and Mrs. Ekman, relations of my Finnish grandmother, wrote that they would be vacationing in Austria and would make a stop to see us in Vöcklabruck on a specific day. They were the first people I would meet who were connected to me through my mother. The relatives I knew were all from my father's side, and since my father and my adoptive mother were brother and sister, I shared those relatives with my siblings. What made me so excited was that these were not typical visitors; they were coming specifically to see me.

All we knew was that they would be arriving in their own car sometime in the afternoon. Grandmother put coal in the stove mid-morning. She had started the yeast dough right after breakfast. Once the yeast had had a chance to rise, she rolled the dough out into a rectangle and covered it with apple slices sprinkled with cinnamon and sugar. I loved the way the house smelled of apples and cinnamon when the apple tart was baking. The plan was to serve coffee and the tart to our visitors. I could not sit still. I kept going outside, coming back in, and asking what time it was.

Taimi and I were outside when we saw a black sedan slowly coming down our street. This had to be them. We ran to the gate and the car slowed, backed up, and then lurched forward, coming to rest halfway on the sidewalk. No one on our street had a car, and parking on the street was not allowed.

Mrs. Ekman did not look the way I had visualized her. In my mind's eye she was tall and slender, with a cape draped over her shoulders and a small hat sporting a feather on her head. Much later I realized that my image was based on a photo I had seen of my mother. The Ekmans were both shorter than I had visualized. Mr. Ekman wore a suit and tie, and Mrs. Ekman wore a solid green dress with an off-white jacket. She came right over to me, taking both of my hands into hers, and said, "Kristina, you look just like your mother."

They brought candy and chocolate for us children. Both were a rare treat for us; Austria was still recovering from the war, and although it was now the late spring of 1949, candy was still hard to get.

I was eager to learn whatever I could about my mother, yet I did not want to ask for information. I sat next to Mrs. Ekman. From her, I learned that my Finnish grandmother was my mother's stepmother and not a blood relative of mine. My actual grandmother had died when my mother was nine years old. I learned that my mother also had an older stepbrother, with whom the Ekmans were not in contact, and that my Finnish grandmother was Mrs. Ekman's aunt.

Most of the talk at the table was among the adults, sharing what their lives had been like since the war began. They asked me about school and told me how much my Finnish grandmother enjoyed getting my letters. I did not like writing to her, since to me she was a stranger. Yet I did enjoy the mail that came from her addressed to me. When the Ekmans left, I wondered if I would ever see them again. I never did, but their son Bertel became a dear friend and for many years my sole connection to my mother's side of the family. In 2009 I met Pia, my mother's half brother's daughter and thus a cousin, with whom I have formed a close relationship.

This visit by the Ekmans made me realize that my life would always have a part that my siblings and I do not share. I had been aware that Grandmother treated me in some ways differently from my siblings, even though they were also her grandchildren. Perhaps she was sensitive to my situation because the loss of my father—her only son—was her loss too. And since I had also lost my mother, she probably felt more of a motherly sense of responsibility for raising me. There were times when she gave me extra treats, acted more protective toward me, and would argue with Mutti on my behalf.

Once, when I was ten years old, I had a bandage on my right eye due to an infection. When I walked out of my school, there was Grandmother to meet me. I was so embarrassed to see her that I stumbled and fell down. I remember thinking she would not have come if Taimi had had a similar infection. My own explanation was that Grandmother felt sorry for me because my parents were dead. Yet, whenever I had angry thoughts about Grandmother, I felt guilty because I also loved her and knew that she loved me.

Since Taimi and I were only seven months apart, for five months of the year we were the same age. Invariably that led to questions as we got older. I would end up explaining that my parents had been killed during the war. This did not seem unusual to my classmates, since many of them had a parent, older brother, or a relative who had not returned from the war. I began to daydream as to what my life might have been like if my parents had lived, imagining scenarios with younger siblings. At the same time I felt that I definitely belonged to my new family and enjoyed having three siblings. After the visit with the Ekmans I decided that I wanted to stay in contact with my mother's side of the family since they were a link to my past.

REX AND THE TEXTILE FACTORY

Rex, our German shepherd, sat up with his ears on alert and began to bark. My brother Hans and I were spending an evening on patrol at the textile factory. When I was about ten years old, Hans, Taimi, and I began doing various jobs that Pappa had assigned to us at the textile factory. Being asked to watch the factory into the night was a new experience for Hans and me. We had assured Pappa that we were up to it.

Rex continued to bark. This night was the annual factory party, and Hans, fifteen, and I, almost thirteen, were in charge of security until Peter, the regular night watchman, returned from celebrating. We had done this job before during the day on weekends, but being there when it was dark outside felt different. When I heard Rex's continuing bark, I found my body stiffening. I don't know if Hans was scared, but he rather casually said, "We better go see what is going on."

We had a regular circuit that we followed and checked off as we walked the premises inside and out. The previous times that evening when we walked the circuit I thought nothing of it. Now that it was close to midnight, and with Rex on the alert, it felt very different. Rex kept growling and Hans followed Rex's lead. Hans held onto the leash and I stayed close behind them. Rex headed straight to the door that led to the canal and turbines.

I whispered to Hans, "What are we going to do if there is someone out there?"

"Rex will protect us," he answered back.

Rex took us across the parking area to the canal. My heart was racing. He sniffed around the grasses, barked as he got to the water's edge, and yanked on the leash. Hans released him from the leash. Rex circled around, barked, and found nothing. We never did know if Rex's loud barking had scared away an intruder or if he had simply heard other animals scampering about.

After two break-ins at the factory, Pappa had decided to get a guard dog. Rex guarded the factory at night and spent the days at our house. In the evenings, Peter, the night watchman, would come to get him, and they would walk to the factory. In the morning, Peter returned him to us. Rex was a handsome German shepherd, with a black body and golden brown face and lower legs. We had never had a pet before and for quite a while I felt scared around this big dog. It took me about six months to be truly comfortable around him. I had heard that he had a history of being mistreated when he was a puppy and that he had been taken to a farm where he had been a good watchdog. When his owners sold their farm, they

With Rex

no longer could keep him. Ever since Rex started his job at the textile factory, there had been no further break-ins.

Peter and his relief watchman and Rex were the best of friends. One New Year's Eve, when the other watchman came to relieve Peter in the middle of the night, Rex had jumped on him. He lunged right for his neck and was ready to bite, when Peter managed to jerk Rex back. This man had alcohol on his breath. The apparent explanation for this unexpected behavior was that Rex must have been abused by his first owner when he was drinking.

Rex's abrupt change in behavior toward the relief night watchman may well have been Rex's instinctive protective response.

One morning, when we were in the kitchen having breakfast, Rex suddenly sat up, stared straight at the door and began to growl. When Taimi walked in, Rex lunged toward her and tried to grab her neck. Grandmother managed to yank him back while screaming: "Get out Taimi! Get out!" Then I too smelled the perfume she had applied that morning. Grandmother went into the hall and hugged Taimi, who was shaking from the experience, and told her to wash off the perfume. Rex quickly settled down under the kitchen table, his favorite spot. When Taimi returned, having totally removed the perfume, Rex was his normal, docile, loving self with her. We learned that strong perfume, like alcohol, was a trigger for Rex.

I liked working at the factory and we had regular summer jobs there. In addition, my girlfriend lived close to the factory, and I usually spent some time hanging out with her. Our earliest jobs at the factory were taking the empty cones that had held the weaving thread and putting them together into long tubes. These tubes were sent back to the supplier to be reused. That was piecemeal work and Taimi and I would challenge each other to see who could do more as we worked on this tedious task. Depending on the job, we reported to the bookkeeper the work completed or the hours the job took. We were paid every two weeks. We even learned to operate some simple machines for carding wool.

When I started seventh grade, we had to write the annual return-to-school essay about our summer vacation. I still have a copy. I began by talking about taking a trip to Salzburg, visiting the World Scout Jamboree, climbing mountains, and going to various lakes. I concluded by saying emphatically that none of these compared with the excitement of spending a day in the yarn-dyeing room at the factory.

I had, for a long time, wanted to be present on a day when the workers colored the skeins of thread. Pappa wanted me to wait until I was older, but finally he gave me permission to join the dyeing team. Early one morning we all put on heavy rubber boots, covered ourselves with big rubber aprons, and got to work. We took plain cotton skeins of thread and colored some batches grey and others red to be woven into fabric for mattress covers. We put the plain colored thread through different baths with the color and the rinse, then put it into the centrifuge to remove the water, and finally hung the freshly colored batches to dry. I kept up with the heavy work of swishing the skeins back and forth in the baths and made sure to do all the other tasks in the dyeing process. We worked late into the afternoon until the job was finished.

Yarn dyeing at the factory

As I think back, I wonder why this was such a special day for me. It must have been because I found the whole process of making fabric fascinating. I had spent time in the weaving room watching as the machines wove the threads into fabric.

Initially these fabrics were for mattress covers, but later the factory made fine fabrics for suits and dresses and table linen. Coloring yarn was another important piece in the process of making clothes. I found out that this step involved a lot of physical labor. Although I enjoyed my day, I never asked to do it again.

Then I fell into a job that ended up being my favorite. I did not look at it as having started a business, but in retrospect I see now that that is exactly what I did.

I knew all the people who worked at the factory—there must have been about 40. A few workers periodically asked me if I would go to a nearby store and buy lunch for them. I was happy to do it. When Pappa found out about it, he was supportive and offered me the use of the three-wheeled bicycle on the premises. In the front it had a big wooden basket that I used as my shopping cart and delivery wagon. The rest was up to me.

Annika is in the basket of the bicycle I used for my lunch business.

Monday through Saturday the factory worked two shifts. Twice every day I ran through the factory floor, ringing a big cowbell. This was the signal that I would be coming around to take orders. I followed this up by walking past every loom and asking the employees for their orders. Besides food I brought beer and *most*, a fermented apple cider that is a well-loved Austrian drink. There was no age limit for buying liquor.

Once I had the orders, I went shopping at several stores. When I returned I handed every person his or her food and collected whatever was owed me. People tipped me generously and I received a minimal hourly wage at the factory. Some days I had many customers, other days only a few. After a while I decided to operate the "lunch canteen" on Monday, Wednesday, and Friday. That gave me more flexibility and people could plan accordingly.

I really enjoyed running the canteen lunch service. I come from a family of enterprising businessmen. As I look back, I see that Mutti and Pappa did not encourage us children to consider business as a career. I do not know if I would have, but I definitely recall that we were discouraged from going into business. Mutti and Pappa, based on their experiences, whether due to economic upheaval or the vagaries of war, saw business as risky. Mutti talked about how hard it was for her to see her father's successes turn to business losses and to see this cycle repeated.

When I read my grandfather's memoir about his business endeavors, I recognized that his views on business entrepreneurship were quite different. He considered the downs as new opportunities to climb to the top. But he never had the state forcibly take over his business, which is what happened to Pappa when the Soviets first occupied Estonia in 1940. Pappa and Mutti thus were much more apprehensive about careers in business.

LAST YEAR IN VÖCKLABRUCK

Austria had become my new homeland. Although I thought of myself as Estonian, I became aware that I felt Austrian too. It had happened gradually, but now that I was twelve, I felt very much at home there. I still remembered living in Estonia, but Estonia and World War II were becoming distant memories. The railroad tracks and bombed buildings near us were long since rebuilt, and finding food was no longer a concern. My family at home continued to speak Estonian. With my friends, I spoke the local German dialect, while in school we spoke High German, which is the unifying language of the country.

As far as we knew, we were the only Estonian family in Vöcklabruck, but Pappa located two other Estonian families in nearby towns. One family had two girls close to my age and we always had fun when we got together. When the Estonian friends visited us, the talk during the course of the evening invariably gravitated to the pros and cons of leaving Austria. President Harry S. Truman had signed the Displaced Persons Act of 1948, giving 400,000 European refugees the opportunity to enter the United States, provided they had a sponsor who would guarantee a job and a place to live. We all had DP identification cards stating that we were eligible for resettlement to countries that would open their doors to refugees. My family understood that the Soviet Union viewed Estonians as their property, but living in the American zone protected us from repatriation. My parents and their friends were all trying to decide where to go. For us children the answer was easy: we wanted to go to America. The Americans were my heroes. They had saved us from the Russian Bear!

Age 12 in Austria

My United Nations identification card

By 1951 the world knew that the Soviet Union had not honored the agreements it made at the conclusion of the war. The Russians were primarily interested in furthering the spread of communism. Initially the Soviet Union had received gratitude and recognition for its part in defeating Nazi Germany. Stalin was also a major player with Churchill and Roosevelt in reestablishing postwar order in Europe, but it did not take long for the world to see that, although the Soviet Union had agreed to grant independence and free elections in the countries under its jurisdiction, none of that happened. The countries that remained under Soviet domination soon found themselves without freedoms. Directed from Moscow, communist parties assumed power in these countries, and any semblance of democracy was annihilated. Three such countries—Czechoslovakia, Hungary, and Yugoslavia— bordered Austria. To my parents, who remembered life under the communists after the Russian invasion of 1940, this was an ever-present concern. They continued to explore the possibility of finding a sponsor in the United States. During 1951 our Estonian friends in the neighboring town had moved to the United States, and the other Estonian family had made New Zealand their new home.

My aunt Liidi urged Grandmother to come to Sweden for a visit. She easily received an entry visa to Sweden, but it took a long time to get an exit visa. Vienna was still divided into four military zones and all four powers had to sign the visa. As it turned out, the Russians refused to sign. The way around this problem was that Grandmother, now 65, had to be accompanied by a "tour guide." Although I was only twelve, when my name was added as the tour guide, she received the requisite signed paper. I felt that I was up to the task of making sure that Grandmother and I made it to Sweden and back. It meant missing school all of April and May, which I did not mind. I greatly looked forward to making this visit, but I was concerned that I would miss the end-of-the-year class trip. I asked my homeroom teacher to please wait for my return and was assured that they would.

Aunt Liidi was a physician in Varberg, a lovely little town on the western coast of Sweden. My two cousins, Juhan and Margus, were seven and nine, and they were not interested in having me around. One of the big differences I noted between us in Austria and our relatives in Sweden was that they had many Estonian friends.

Visiting Aunt Liidi in Sweden.
Front row: Cousin Juhan, Aunt Liidi Mägi, Cousin Margus, and me. Back row: Uncle Arvo Mägi, Hans Lellep, Grandmother Linda Lellep Luts, Heino Lellep.

Uncle Arvo Mägi was a writer and journalist active in the Estonian community in Sweden. It was hard to get any credible information from Estonia, because all correspondence was censored. I don't know how they did it, but Uncle Arvo and his colleagues did seem to obtain news. They kept the West informed of life under the Soviets in Estonia.

At my aunt's house, with friends who stopped by and with Grandmother, everyone talked about the plight of the people left behind and how horrific life was for them under communism. People in Estonia had limited means and were under constant surveillance, never knowing when something about them would be reported to the authorities. A frightening purge had occurred two years before, in 1949. Without any warning or reason, during three days the Soviets deported more than 20,000 Estonians, mainly women and children, to Siberia. The Estonians in Sweden were sending relief packages to families back home, never knowing if the packages arrived or were confiscated. I was glad that we had gotten out of Estonia and were living in Austria.

While I was in Sweden, one of the families we had gotten to know moved to Canada. They were approved because they were displaced from their homeland, Estonia. It surprised me that they chose to leave Sweden since Sweden, which had been a neutral country during the war, at least seemed a safe and thriving place to be. To me it made more sense that my parents in Austria were looking into finding a permanent home in another country.

I also took a trip to visit my godparents in a town about four hours away by train. They had both been close friends of my biological parents in Viljandi. Aunt Maja, at my mother's urging, had also come to Estonia from Finland and, while there, met and married Uncle Evald Treffner, my father's good friend. They showed me photos and told me stories of good times they had shared. My mother had loved to entertain, and it seemed that they had a group of friends visit most weekends. My parents' deaths had left a terrible void in the hearts and lives of their friends.

When I returned to Austria from Sweden I noticed a curious change in my friends. Suddenly much of their talk centered on boys. This had not been a topic between us before. My friends couldn't wait to tell me about the cute boys they were meeting after school and on weekends. Several of them swooned over one boy in particular. Although they were glad to see me, they were much more interested in telling me about their new interests than in hearing about my trip. I was taken aback and felt left out since boys were not yet on my personal radar. The boys I knew were my brother's friends, and we paid no attention to each other. This new world my friends had entered upset me for about six months, and then I found myself joining them eagerly in this new preoccupation.

As promised, my classmates and teacher had waited for my return from Sweden before taking the annual class trip. Our destination was the charming lakeside town of St. Wolfgang, where we visited the local church with the famous Gothic altarpiece completed by Michael Pacher in 1481. I stood there in awe of the intricately carved altar, which reached almost from the floor to the ceiling, with painted wing panels that were closed at certain times of the year. It was evident that our teacher loved this altar. Her detailed descriptions made a lasting impression, and I was thrilled that they had waited for me. Although I was an average student, I loved going to school and enjoyed my friends and learning.

My parents were eager for us children to play an instrument. Taimi started with the piano. She practiced at two different families' homes since we did not have a piano. Pappa had purchased a violin for his pleasure. He loved playing when Estonian friends came, concluding an evening with Estonian songs followed by singing the Estonian National Anthem.

Our parents suggested that Hans and I take violin lessons. I was unhappy because that was not the instrument I wanted to play. The instrument I liked best was the Alpine zither, which my girlfriend's father often played when I visited her. He had me try this instrument, which is generally played on a table and has strings on a sounding box. I found it difficult to get the notes right, but I loved the sound I produced. As I look back I realize that I never told my parents of my interest. I had a real appreciation for music and loved to sing, but knew that the violin would be hard for me. I did not have a natural ear for music, whereas Pappa did. Whenever he was home and heard me practicing, he found it excruciating. I can still hear him calling out to me from the other room: "Too high ... too low." I could not hear the difference and found the whole experience frustrating. I took lessons from my music teacher, a woman I loved dearly. She was much more positive, but I was self-conscious whenever I had to play for Pappa the piece that I had been practicing. Pappa's voice had become my voice; I kept repeating to myself, "too high ... too low," not really knowing which it was.

At the end of the school year, the music students put on a concert. The school choir sang several songs. Then it was time for the quartet, of which I was a member, to play. We were two violins and two violas. We took our positions, bowed, and sat down. We started playing in unison. I looked like I was playing intently, but my bow never touched a string. I was so worried that I would spoil our piece. I was convinced that being too high and too low would be evident to the audience. I felt ashamed of my playing and did not want anyone else to know that I could not tell when I was slightly off-key. When we rehearsed, my teacher had been positive about how our quartet played together. There was enthusiastic clapping after our piece. I did not know what to make of it when no one remarked that I had not really played. I was sure the audience had noticed and kept wondering what they really thought of me.

Maybe I can't forget this incident because there have been other times when I was convinced of an outcome without daring to find out what really would happen if I followed through. I did realize that what I said to myself had everything to do with what I was willing to do. I talked myself out of touching the bow to the strings. Yes, I was scared, shy and self-conscious, but it was Pappa's voice that echoed in my ears and immobilized me. This incident also made me aware that what I did was not acceptable. I did not like it that I was so scared of making a mistake that I refused to even try. Soon thereafter I stopped playing the violin. Then my sister Annika began to study the violin and luckily for her she had Pappa's ear for music.

After considerable deliberation, our parents began the process of applying for a sponsorship to the United States. Pappa was uneasy about taking this step because the textile factory under his leadership was doing well. He worried what life would be like for him in a country where he hardly knew the language and he was already in his early 40s. Mutti, who spoke English, was much more positive. Yet for both of them the final decision came down to the fact that they felt that living in America would provide a better future for us children. Our first sponsorship offer came from an orange grower in Cucamonga, California. Mutti had visions that we children would have to pick oranges instead of going to school. My parents turned this offer down. I do not remember what the second offer was, but again my parents said no. They were beginning to wonder if they were cutting off their opportunity to get to America by continuing to refuse the offers.

One day two ladies affiliated with the Lutheran World Federation stopped by. They said they would find a sponsor for us. They carried a big binder with a page and picture of each family they were trying to place and our information was added to it. After a number of months they came back with a sponsorship offer from St. Peter's Lutheran Church in Allentown, Pennsylvania. The pastor, Dr. Hagen Staack, had come there from Germany after the war and had a bilingual English/German congregation in Allentown. He was interested in getting additional German-speaking families for his congregation. He had found us by paging through the binder compiled by the Lutheran World Federation. This offer sounded much better than the others and my parents accepted it. After Christmas 1951 we met with the U.S. consul in Salzburg and were approved to begin our journey in the beginning of the New Year. We were going to America.

LEAVING AUSTRIA

We had lived in Vöcklabruck, Austria, since the fall of 1944, arriving there eight months before World War II ended. (Occupation finally ended in 1955, three years after we had left.) Now it was 1952. Vöcklabruck had become our home, and especially in the past four years, life had been good for our family. We took advantage of the beauty that surrounded us by exploring the spectacular mountains and lakes nearby. I learned to love the music of the Austrian composers Mozart, Strauss, Schubert, Bruckner, and Haydn. They are all still favorites. I do not remember how I learned to waltz and polka but, looking back, it seems I always knew.

Our sponsors in the United States guaranteed that they would help find employment and housing for us. We were excited to be going to America. Once our family accepted this offer, we had about a month to prepare for our departure. For the past half year I had been immersing myself in reading books by American authors. My favorites were *Tom Sawyer* and *Huckleberry Finn*, which I obtained at the library. As excited as I was to move to this land of skyscrapers and cowboys, I was also sad to leave my friends and our familiar way of life. On my last day in school my classmates sang a beautiful farewell song for me. During the last stanza many of my classmates burst into tears. I did not cry, but I had the overwhelming feeling that this was the last time that I would ever see my friends and teachers and be part of life in the town that I had learned to love.

Monday, January 21, 1952, was our last morning in Vöcklabruck. After the truck was loaded with all our boxes I walked once more through the house that had been my home for almost four years. For days I had been worried what would happen to Rex if a new home were not found for him. Finally, the day before we were leaving, a couple who had a farm stopped by to see Rex and quickly decided that they would take him. It was sad to say goodbye to him.

My three closest girlfriends came to see me off. We giggled and laughed and kept promising each other that we would stay in touch. None of us wanted to admit the sadness we felt just beneath our overly good mood. The presence of my three friends helped to make the departure easier for me. We drove away amidst much waving, and I kept repeating quietly to myself, "I will be back."

As it turned out, I did return in 2008, and my classmates organized a class reunion. I had remained in contact with my classmate Helga Wimberger and she was instrumental in getting us all together. Even my homeroom teacher, then 90 years old, attended. Although we all had changed over the years, we enjoyed remembering the times we had shared as children.

The first part of our journey from Vöcklabruck took us to Salzburg, where we stayed in a modern hotel for three days. Our family occupied three beautiful rooms, each with a bath. After all the years of going to the public baths, this was a real luxury. Mutti and Pappa met with the Lutheran World Federation to settle on the logistics for our trip.

On our last day in Salzburg, I took a bus with Taimi to go to some shops and look around. We had a good time, but somehow became separated. I ran back to places we had been, but did not find her.

It began to get dark, and I decided that I had better return to the hotel. I thought I knew exactly where I was going. As we left the city behind, I realized I had taken the wrong bus. We were headed in the opposite direction from where I needed to be. At the next stop, I was astounded to find that we were near the Hellbrunn Palace, famous for its fountains. We had visited there the previous summer and it had seemed so far out of the city. I asked the driver if he was going to go back to the city. He answered that he had to make a few more stops, but that he would not be returning to Salzburg. He pointed across a snowy field to distant lights. There, he said, I would be able to catch a bus back to the city. As I trudged through the snow, I was upset with myself that I had taken the wrong bus. I stopped at a farmhouse and a store for directions. I finally found a bus and made my way back to the hotel.

When I arrived, the whole family, including Taimi, was in the dining room eating dinner. Mutti asked inquisitively, "Where have you been?" I said, "I took the wrong bus." I joined them at the table. We talked a little about my experience. What amazed me was that no one, not even Grandmother, appeared to have been anxious about my absence. I did not let on that, when I stopped at the farmhouse, I was scared and worried whether I would find my way back. I was so relieved to be reunited. Then it occurred to me that perhaps they were not concerned about my absence because they trusted that I would find my way back to the hotel. And indeed I had managed to do so. This was our last night in Austria. The next morning we were leaving by train for Bremerhaven, Germany, where we would begin our journey across the Atlantic Ocean to America.

MY FRIEND HAROLD

When we arrived in Bremerhaven, we learned we had at least a two-week wait. We were assigned to barracks-type housing that we shared with several other families at a military camp. February 1952 was cold and snowy. I remember little about how we lived there, but remember well my friendship with Harold. His family consisted of his aunt, two older women, and several young men who slept in the male quarters. Harold was thirteen years old, like me, and we formed a special friendship. He did not pal around with my brother or my sisters except when we all played games in the evening. He and I liked spending time with each other and talking.

As we got to know each other, I asked him where his parents were. He told me that he had not seen his parents since he was three years old. He did not know where they were and had heard that they might be dead, but no one really seemed to know. I told him that I had lost my parents during the war and that I knew that mine were dead. He said to me, "Sometimes I imagine what my life would be like if they were still around." I understood what he was saying. I told him that I also thought about that, but had never before shared it with anyone else.

One day Taimi asked me, "Why are you always hanging out with him? Come do something with me."

"I like being with him," I answered.

This was my first friendship with a boy. When Harold and I walked, we held hands. We had fun together. We explored the huge military campground, went to movies shown in a big hall, and even took part in a "learn to speak English" class.

What we enjoyed the most was just talking and being with each other. He had a wonderful imagination and regaled me with stories. We assumed that we would be on the same ship crossing the ocean.

Then his family learned that they would be departing the following day. I had known Harold for seven days. We were both sad that we would not be on the same ship. Harold promised, "I will definitely be there to meet you when your boat comes into New York harbor." I told him that would make me very happy. We both knew that there was little chance of ever seeing each other again.

I was sad when my friend left for New York City, where he said they had relatives. Later I overheard people say that the family that just left was Jewish. Harold had never mentioned that he was Jewish. I wondered if Harold's parents perished in a concentration camp, how Harold escaped, whether the people he was with were really his aunt and extended family, and how they survived. I knew that my mother died when the Russians shot down the plane *Kaleva* on her flight from Estonia to Finland. And I knew that my father, a soldier in the German army, died in Latvia when his motorcycle hit a land mine. Harold could only imagine what might have happened to his parents. Both of our lives were torn apart by the cruel ambitions of Stalin and Hitler.

GOING TO AMERICA

On February 11, 1952, we at last boarded the USNS *General M. B. Stewart* for our voyage across the Atlantic Ocean. Our ship had transported soldiers during the war and now was carrying displaced persons to America. Women and men were housed in separate parts of the ship. Mutti and we three girls were assigned to F Deck with 300 other people deep inside the bowels of the ship. There was a scramble for beds. We located two across from each other that would accommodate us. Each bed unit was designed as four vertical bunk beds. We used the upper bunk for our luggage and slept on the middle two rope beds; we placed our shoes on the bottom one. Grandmother, being older, had quarters that were slightly more comfortable.

USNS General M. B. Stewart (T-AP-140) was used after the war to transport displaced persons.

I was seasick during the first couple of days, but then became used to the constant swaying of the ship. We were told that the best remedy for seasickness was to be sure to eat, which was the last thing I wanted to do. Breakfast started at 7 a.m., our midday meal was at 11 a.m., and dinner was at 4:30 p.m. I liked spending as much time as possible outside because the air was stuffy in our crowded quarters. There were a lot of people speaking many different languages. I met one girl, close to my age, part of a group of about 15 children, most of them younger than she. They were all traveling together with several adults. They were orphans who had been moved from Germany to England during the war. She excitedly told me that they all would be getting new families in America.

On our sixth day out at sea, the weather changed. The wind howled and grew in intensity. The ship groaned and heaved. In the mess hall, the food sloshed from one end of the long metal tables to the other. At one point the angle of the ship tilted so abruptly that it tossed me right out of my seat.

There was always a pot of coffee on each table. During this fierce storm, coffee pots and plates full of food would crash to the floor. For years afterwards, the smell of coffee upset me. During the storm, all the doors to the outside had to be kept closed. No one was permitted to go on deck. Being confined with all those people with no fresh air was, for me, the toughest part of our ocean crossing.

The wind rose to hurricane strengths, delaying our arrival by two days and prolonging the journey to New York to a total of ten days. We heard that a large freighter had broken in half by being tossed around in the storm. At last the wind and rain died down, and we could venture on deck again. During our final two days, everyone on board was processed for admission to the United States. Our entire family had to be present for our turn. At one point, we were told the names of various organizations that we could not join in the United States. My parents signed a paper indicating they would abide by this order. Curiously, they never received a copy of what they had signed.

After what seemed like a never-ending trip we were told to be on deck the following morning at 3 a.m. for our arrival in New York City. I don't think Taimi and I slept at all. We were able to get a spot at the railing on the right side of the ship. Many people were already on deck. It was still dark. Not being sure of what we were seeing, we at first spotted what appeared to be faint lights in the distance. As we got closer and dawn came, we made out that the lights belonged to skyscrapers slowly rising through the morning haze. I had seen the New York skyline in photos, but to actually see the immensity of the buildings as approached from the ocean was a magical experience. To me, this was my image of America.

Mutti came rushing over to where we were standing. "Hurry, you have to come to the other side," she said breathlessly. We heard a multitude of voices becoming louder and louder. And then I saw her. She was huge. Our ship was passing an enormous statue of a woman wearing a crown on her head and holding a torch. People were pointing to her, hugging each other, lifting up their children, calling out in different languages. I saw several women on their knees raising up their arms and thanking God. It was then that I learned that this was the Statue of Liberty welcoming us all. I had not known of her before. I can still see the sun coming up and the Statue shimmering in the morning light. After all the many days of rain and wind and cold and the many years of being displaced persons, we had at last arrived. The day was February 22 in 1952, which was a national holiday honoring George Washington, the first president of the United States. We were in America.

KALEVA REVISITED

The United States has been my home since we arrived here in 1952 as displaced persons. Five years after we came to the United States, we became naturalized citizens in our new hometown, Allentown, Pennsylvania. The ceremony took place in a stately park with tall trees and beautiful beds of roses and varied flowers. I had walked across the same stage a week earlier and received my high school graduation diploma. The band played patriotic music, and the mayor and other dignitaries proudly welcomed us to this great country. When our group of about 25 immigrants said the Pledge of Allegiance, we received a standing ovation accompanied by loud cheers from the flag-waving crowd. We were now Americans after years of being exiles without an official homeland. Yet we continued to think of ourselves as Estonian-Americans. And then, unexpectedly and years later, I was pulled back to where my story began in 1940, when the Russians shot down the *Kaleva* airplane in which my mother perished.

Ants Vist, an Estonian film producer making a documentary on the *Kaleva,* contacted me in 2006. He came to our home in Annapolis, Maryland, and interviewed me for the film. For several years I heard nothing from him, and I began to wonder if the documentary would ever be finished. Then I found out that Ants Vist had been severely injured and required a long recovery; one of his colleagues completed the project.

One afternoon there was a knock on our front door and I received a package sent from Estonia by Helin Roop, a dear relative. I eagerly opened the package not knowing what to expect. Inside were two chocolate bars, a lovely Estonian calendar, and a DVD. I looked at the cover and my heart began to race. I saw an airplane with "OH-ALL KALEVA" written on its side and the title, *The Mystery of the Kaleva.*

I inserted the DVD, but could not get it to play. I tried a different player with the same result. I had run into similar situations before: most European DVDs are programmed so they do not play on U.S. players. Finally I called my granddaughter Kirsten, who suggested I try my laptop. I was riveted as *The Mystery of the Kaleva* began to play. I was surprised how anxious I felt. During the three days that Ants Vist and the photographer spent at our house they filmed me a number of times, asking questions about my mother. I was curious to see how the story would unfold and how they had used the material that I shared.

The film began by describing the political situation in Europe in June 1940. I was impressed by the extensive search to find the wreckage of the *Kaleva* and the intensity with which the researcher Toivo Kallas, who has no personal connection to the *Kaleva,* was determined to find the place where the plane went down. He hoped that when the plane was brought to the surface the mystery of why the *Kaleva* was shot down would be revealed. As the movie proceeded, there was an extensive interview with the son of the pilot. He and I, since we were so young, have no personal recollection of the parents we lost. The discussions between the interviews focus on various hypotheses why the *Kaleva* was attacked. Suddenly I saw a familiar photo of my mother. It covered the whole screen. She looked lovely, being only 24 years old. I had given a copy of this photo to the director, but it was different to see her here as part of the story that explored the fate of the *Kaleva.* Next there was a photo of my parents and me. And then the camera shifted to Ants Vist interviewing me in Annapolis.

I am sitting on our deck overlooking Back Creek in Annapolis, Maryland. I am speaking Estonian. English sub-titles translate what I am saying. My apprehension lifts as I hear myself talk. I realize that I was anxious because I hoped I would come across in a way that reflected well on my mother and on me, her daughter. I am also impressed that my Estonian sounds so good.

Much to my surprise, the next person interviewed is my Aunt Liidi in Sweden, who at the time of the filming must have been in her late 80s. She has died since, at the age of 95, which makes it even more special to see her here. She is the person who, as an exchange student in Finland, met my mother and subsequently invited her to Estonia, where she fell in love with my father, her brother.

The film goes on to explore the five different theories why the plane may have been targeted. The documentary describes in detail the searches with underwater robots looking for the plane on the seabed. There were six different attempts to find the *Kaleva*. The last one was with the help of the United Sates Navy oceanographic survey ship *Pathfinder,* using sophisticated sonar equipment.

But after all these thorough searches, the *Kaleva* was not found. The documentary finally concludes that we may never know definitively why the Russians targeted the *Kaleva*. Was it just a brazen display of Russian power to show a small country that it was powerless on the world stage? Or did the Russians want to intercept sensitive materials that were being taken out of the country? No relatives of the German and French passengers have been located, and no one knows why. Where they spies? Did they use aliases? Some of the mystery still remains.

For me the loss was personal. Although my mother died, she has remained in many ways a part of my life. I have tangible items—some of her jewelry and silverware and relatives in Finland that the rest of my siblings do not share. I was an only child adopted into my father's sister's family, which gave me three siblings. I am in many ways like them, and yet different. I remember feeling, from the time I was quite young, that I must not bring shame on my parents. That it was up to me to make something of myself. When I was growing up, there were times when I fantasized what my life might have been like if my parents had lived. My mother and father have remained in my heart and pop up in my thoughts unexpectedly. When I got married, had children and then grandchildren and at other times I wished that my parents were here to share these special times with me. I have also felt sad for them because they lost their lives so young.

As a result of growing up during World War II, my life took a different path. I consider myself very fortunate to have been raised by Mutti and Pappa, by whom I felt greatly loved, and to have three incredible siblings. At the same time I am aware that my life has been lived under the shadows cast by Stalin and Hitler and that the war they started caused me to lose my parents and my homeland, Estonia.

TRIP TO KERI ISLAND

Ever since I heard that Finland had erected a memorial to the *Kaleva*, I longed to visit Keri Island, the piece of land closest to where the *Kaleva* plunged into the Gulf of Finland. In the summer of 2013, my husband, Tycho, our son Erik, his wife Betty, and children, Lily, 9, and James, 8, and I took a trip to Estonia. In addition to visiting relatives, exploring Tallinn, and returning to Viljandi, I wanted to visit Keri Island. The day we had planned for our trip to Keri Island was windy and too treacherous for the voyage. We would have to try another day.

Three days in a row I anxiously called the harbormaster of the only company that I had found that would take passengers to the island. Each time I was hoping to hear that today would be the day that we could take our boat trip to Keri Island. The answer was the same: "The weather is too dangerous. There are fierce winds and treacherous waves." Then on the last possible day for us, since we were heading back to the United States the following morning, the weather finally broke in the early afternoon and I was told: "Be here at 4 o'clock."

It's a 14-mile boat ride from Tallinn across the Gulf of Finland toward Helsinki, Finland. We put on warm jackets. Lily and James fuss about having to wear snowsuits in the summer. We fasten life jackets over our clothes. The boat is a 30-foot inflatable rubber boat with a captain and a mate. We jump down into the boat and mount the two rows of seats upon which we sit as if riding a horse. The captain warns us that we have to hold on tightly since this will be a rough, cold ride lasting close to an hour.

We launch. The small boat first lifts its bow and then settles down to plane on the surface of the water. We skim across the water at a fast clip. Our path takes us past two islands out into the Gulf of Finland. All I can see is water. The captain holds a steady course. There is no sign of land anywhere. I am getting anxious. This trip is important to me.

On the way to Keri Island.
Front row: James and Erik. Middle: Betty and Lily. Back row: Tycho and me

I am now on my way to the land closest to where the remains of my mother are. Suddenly, way in the distance, I glimpse what appears to be a change on the horizon. There is something ahead that could be a speck of land. As we get closer, I make out a lighthouse and know that this is Keri Island. I had been warned that we might not be able to land, since the pier had been torn apart during recent winters.

We arrive at the island, and our captain and his mate, Victor, explore the rocky coast, assessing if there is a spot where they may safely pull the boat ashore. They understand how important it is to me to get onto the island. Victor puts on a wetsuit and slides into the water. On his first attempt to get us ashore, he concludes that the shoreline is too steep and rocky. By now Victor is waist high in the water pulling our boat. We are all worried that, after getting so close, we may have to abandon our plan to go ashore.

At last he finds a safe place, and with joy and relief we climb out and clamber up the rocks onto the island. I scamper over the stones and grasses covered with wildflowers up the hill toward the lighthouse. To the left of it, near the center of the island, is the *Kaleva* Memorial. It is positioned on an elevated, rectangular grassy area. A modern-looking pyramid made of four metal tubes rises up about 14 feet. Between them is a three-dimensional cross of smaller tubes welded together. In front of the memorial are three plaques written in Finnish. They relate that the *Kaleva* was shot down nearby on June 14, 1940, give the names of the pilot and copilot, show an engraving of the plane high above Keri Island, and give the date, June 14, 1993, when the memorial was erected.

I place a small pot of marigolds before the center plaque. For me it is very special to be here and to share this place with my family. I smell the lovely fragrance of the four lilac bushes in glorious bloom near the memorial. I see this tiny island, barely seven acres, as a beautiful place of remembrance of the passengers who lost their lives on the *Kaleva*. Sadly, since the lighthouse was automated in 2002, there has no longer been public boat access to the island.

We walk around this peaceful island. We are the only people here. Among the tall grasses are specks of blue, pink and yellow flowers whose names I do not know. There is a low building on the other end of the island where the lighthouse keeper must have lived. The maintenance people who come to the island periodically probably use it now. I can tell that someone has been here recently, because the grass around the memorial has been cut. The door is unlocked and we decide to enter. To our delight we find a cardboard box filled with brand new glass mugs with an etching of Keri Island based on a design from 1939. There is a small sign indicating how much they cost. We buy several glasses by leaving the right amount of money in a jar next to them. There is a logbook on the table. I write in Estonian that I was here with my family to visit the *Kaleva* Memorial and to pay tribute to my mother and all who perished on this airplane.

At the *Kaleva* memorial on Keri Island

As we leave the building, we roll a couple of stones against the door to keep it shut, just the way we found it. I stop by the memorial for a last look. I am thankful to the Finns for having memorialized the brutal attack on the *Kaleva*. I think about what it must have been like for the nine people on the *Kaleva* when they realized what was happening. Just as I have never forgotten my mother, it means a lot to me that after all these years the attack on the *Kaleva* continues to be remembered in Estonian and Finnish World War II history as a significant event. A slight wind and warm sunshine surround me. We head back to the boat. I am at peace, realizing how blessed I have been in spite of this tragedy early in my life.

EPILOGUE AND ACKNOWLEDGMENTS

The Russian Bear, asleep for so long, seems to have reawakened. I had not worried about him since coming to the United States. I was thrilled when Estonia regained its independence in 1991 and could leave behind the communist way of life that had been forced upon it.

In the summer of 2014, Russian President Vladimir Putin claimed Crimea and invaded eastern Ukraine. This was followed by the crash of the Malaysian airplane MH17 in Ukraine, initially considered an accident. Later reports alleged that the civilian aircraft was shot down by pro-Russian insurgents firing a Russian air missile. This action to me was reminiscent of what happened to the *Kaleva* in 1940, now 75 years ago. Again there were the Russian denials of having had anything to do with this "accident." I fervently hope that the world will contain the Russian Bear and not allow it to expand its reach by force.

I decided to write my memoir because I wanted to share my experiences of what it was like to be a child during World War II and its aftermath. It also was important to me as an adult to understand the turbulent political situation as it had affected my life. My view as a little girl was simple: the Russian Bear was trying to capture us. It was later that I learned that the Russian Bear also represented communism and that our escapes were fueled by a longing to live free.

In 2012 I joined a memoir-writing class in Annapolis. I am grateful to my teacher, Janice Gary, and my astute classmates for their helpful observations, unfailing interest in my story, and encouragement to write what became *Escaping the Russian Bear*.

As I look back on my life, I see how important it has been to have had the help of so many caring people. First I had the love of my aunt and uncle, who adopted me and became my new parents. When it came to escaping from Estonia as the Russians occupied the country in 1944, we had a letter written by Mr. Mayerhofer to his father-in-law, Mr. Czerwenka, asking him to give us refuge in Austria. This generous act made all the difference in our lives. When we needed a sponsor in order to come to the United States, Dr. Hagen Staack and the congregation of St. Peter's Lutheran Church in Allentown, Pennsylvania, made it possible. They were instrumental in easing the transition to our new homeland. The American dream—that working hard would lead to endless opportunities—was liberating and a great motivator for us children.

My siblings, Hans, Taimi, and Annika, have ardently encouraged my writing. Our talks together have helped refresh my memory and correct errors of fact. We all realize how fortunate we were to have had caring parents and a loving grandmother and to have so many good memories of the tumultuous years of war and its aftermath.

I am most grateful to my husband, Tycho, for his love and support throughout my writing and our life together. His twin brother, Christian, graciously shared his expertise in editing and manuscript preparation and was unfailingly supportive. I thank my publisher, P. Aarne Vesilind of Lakeshore Press, for his invaluable help in creating this book and in believing that my memoir is an important contribution to Estonian World War II history. I also thank my manuscript readers, whose helpful input I have greatly appreciated.

My children and their spouses, Hille and Chris, Tycho and Alison, and Erik and Betty, have all urged me to tell my story. Recently my granddaughter Cecilia, working on a class project asked me, "Did you get any food from UNICEF when you were a child during World War II?" Indeed, UNICEF and other organizations for a while were our lifeline for food.

I hope that my memoir will give my grandchildren, Cecilia, Thomas, Kirsten, Tycho, Lily, and James, and all who read *Escaping the Russian Bear,* a better understanding of the politics and human toll of war when I, and millions of people like me, were caught up in Stalin and Hitler's battle for dominance during World War II. We fortunately succeeded in outrunning the Russian Bear, whose big claw had been poised to grab us and forcibly take us back to Estonia to decide our fate.